THE EMPEROR'S
LAST ISLAND

Julia Blackburn is the author of *Charles Waterton, The Emperor's Last Island, Daisy Bates in the Desert*, which was shortlisted for the Waterstones/Esquire/Volvo Non-Fiction Award, and *The Book of Colour*, which was shortlisted for the Orange Prize for Fiction. She lives in Suffolk with her two children.

Julia Blackburn

THE EMPEROR'S LAST ISLAND

A Journey to St Helena

VINTAGE

Published by Vintage 1997

8 10 9 7

Lines from 'Away, Melancholy' by Stevie Smith
(*The Collected Poems of Stevie Smith*,
Penguin 20th Century Classics)
reprinted with kind permission of the executor, James MacGibbon

First published in Great Britain by
Martin Secker & Warburg Ltd, 1991

Vintage
Random House, 20 Vauxhall Bridge Road, London SW1V 2SA
www.rbooks.co.uk

Addresses for companies within
The Random House Group Limited can be found at:
www.randomhouse.co.uk/offices.htm

The Random House Group Limited Reg. No. 954009

A CIP catalogue record for this book
is available from the British Library

ISBN 9780099752110

Penguin Random House is committed to a sustainable future for
our business, our readers and our planet. This book is made from
Forest Stewardship Council® certified paper.

Printed and bound in Great Britain by Clays Ltd, Elcograf S.p.A.

For Hein, with love

Contents

Acknowledgements

I would like to thank the Author's Foundation at the Society of Authors for giving me a generous travel grant at a time when it seemed impossible to arrange the journey to St Helena.

Trevor Hearl, a long-standing friend of St Helena and its people, provided me with a great deal of information about the island's complicated past history and its present developments.

The London Library was the chief source for the books and periodicals I have consulted in London. In France I was most grateful for the help of M. Chevallier and M. Pougetoux at the Musée National du Château de Malmaison.

The people of St Helena were hospitable and kind, but I am particularly grateful to George and Coral Moyce; to our neighbours Mary Lawrence and Aubrey and Sonia Lawrence, as well as to Julian Cairns-Wicks at Mount Pleasant and Cecil Maggott, Custodian of Records at the Government Archives in Jamestown.

I would also like to thank Rosalie Blackburn, Basil Saunders, Dan Franklin, Toby Eady and Kiek Droogleever Fortuyn. My husband, Hein Bonger, read the manuscript during the various stages of its development and his comments were always clear and valuable.

Finally I would like to say that my two children, Natasha and Martin Thomas, proved themselves to be enthusiastic travelling companions.

' I could be bounded in a nutshell and count myself a king of infinite space, were it not that I have bad dreams.'

Shakespeare, *Hamlet*

'How far is St Helena from the field of Waterloo?
A near way – a clear way – the ship will take you soon.
A pleasant place for gentlemen with little else to do.'

Rudyard Kipling, 'A St Helena Lullaby'

CHAPTER I

'Are there any lions or tigers about
here?' she asked timidly.
'It's only the Red King snoring,' said
Tweedledee.

Lewis Carroll, *Through the Looking Glass*

When I first started to think about the idea of a man like
Napoleon trapped on an island like St Helena, I was
reminded of an incident I had witnessed many years ago,
on a road in the mountains somewhere in southern Spain.
A small car travelling just ahead of me suddenly crashed
into the large nose of an oncoming lorry. The car contained
three members of the *guardia civil* police force and the
leader of the three men, a colonel distinguished by the
ribbons and medals that decorated his dark uniform, was
sitting in the front passenger seat, so that when the
collision took place he was thrown forward, his head hit
the windscreen and he suffered a mild concussion. The
other two men were unharmed and I watched as they
hurriedly clambered out of the car and began to heave the
passive body of their superior on to the road. His face was

deathly pale, but although it was without expression it still looked rather dangerous, as if the owner might at any moment open his jaws and bite.

Now the two officers obviously had to try to behave correctly in the presence, albeit the unconscious presence, of such an important person, and so instead of leaving him lying there helpless and unattended, they heaved him up from the hot naked road and, with one of them holding him by the feet while the other grasped him under the arms, they went to discuss the accident with the lorry driver. There they stood for what seemed like an interminable length of time, in the heat of the day, with that heavy body hanging between them, the medals glinting lopsidedly in the sun, the socks exposed and a military hat balanced on a gently heaving chest. At last they had worked out who was to be blamed for what and with tottering steps they returned to their car, pulled and pushed the general along the length of the back seat, climbed in themselves and continued on their interrupted journey. It was tempting to think that for a brief moment I had seen the unconscious man open his eyes and stare incredulously at what was taking place, before lapsing back into an uneasy oblivion; but perhaps that was only a trick of the bright sunlight.

And where is Napoleon in all this? He is there in the predicament of the concussed General: dressed in fine clothes and saturated with a smell of power and authority that is as pungent as the scent of a fox, and yet for the six final years of his life helplessly suspended out of time and history; stranded on a tiny volcanic island in the middle of the South Atlantic Ocean.

In 1812, when he was retreating from the blood and confusion of Moscow and the disastrous Russian Campaign, Napoleon had remarked that there was only a single step separating the sublime from the ridiculous. From the moment that he was deposited on St Helena, until the day when his body was finally removed from the island twenty-five years later, the sublime and the ridiculous were often so closely intertwined that it was impossible to separate the one from the other. The servants and companions who were with him on the island still treated him with all the fear and respect that was owing to an emperor, but the more they bobbed and bowed in Napoleon's presence and tried to maintain the illusion of courtly life, the more rigidly they needed to shut out any mirror reflection of what they were doing and how they looked while they were doing it. Similarly, the stream of visitors who stopped off at the island in the hope of catching sight of its famous prisoner, the battalions of soldiers who guarded him, the hierarchy of officials who were organising his captivity, they all in their different ways found it very hard to see Napoleon as he was in this present moment, and not as he once had been, or as he would surely be again if he ever escaped. Even when he was dead, lying there stiff and cold in his uniform, the patient queues of people who came to stare at him approached with extreme caution, as if he might suddenly jump to his feet.

Meanwhile, for six long years, an overweight and middle-aged man sat in a ramshackle house, hemmed in by the heat, the rain and the wind; by rats, by soldiers and by government representatives; and he did his best to encourage the repetitive tedium of his existence to drift from one day into the next. He could spend an entire morning watching the clouds as they moved across the range of mountains in the distance behind his house; he could pick a flower and stare into its bright colours until the people standing around him became uneasy and restless; he would lie in his bath for hours on end and I have been told that when you look at that bath you can see how his hand has worn a smoothness into the shallow dish that used to hold the soap.

I am here concerned with the tangle of stories and myths, the absurdities and simple facts that accumulated around Napoleon while he was living on St Helena, and that went on growing and multiplying long after he was dead and buried in an unmarked grave in a little valley that came to be known as the Valley of the Tomb. And always in the background there is the fact of the island itself, the distant steep-sided stage on which this particular drama was enacted; a place that is said to be more remote than anywhere else on earth.

When Napoleon was first confronted by St Helena, he was shocked by its quality of silence and desolation and the way that it appeared from a distance like a fortress of solid rock. His first impression did not improve or mellow over the years and he grew to hate this island that seemed to mock him with its unyielding indifference, and yet, in certain ways, suffered along with him. I have been told that St Helena today has hardly changed since the time when Napoleon cursed it for its thin soil and sudden mists. Everyone who has been there says that it still carries a sense of being cut off from the rest of the world; a tiny pinnacle of land surrounded by an ocean that seems to have no boundaries; a place that is closed in on itself, preoccupied with the memories of all that it has known and seen. And because Napoleon felt its relentless brooding presence so keenly, the island is as much a part of this story as the man.

CHAPTER II

From the place where we rode, which
was on the northwest side, there is
hardly such another Ragged, steepy,
stony, high, Cragged, rocky, barren,
Desolate, and Comfortless coast to be
seen. But above, the ground is of
excellent Mold.

The Voyage of Peter Mundy

St Helena is further away from anywhere than anywhere
else in all the world. It is a dot in the middle of the South
Atlantic, situated just below the line of the Equator;
eighteen hundred miles from the coast of Brazil in South
America, and twelve hundred miles from the port of
Alexander in Angolan Africa. Even its nearest neighbour,
pale grey and brittle Ascension Island, is separated from it
by seven hundred miles of deep ocean waters.

I have not yet been to St Helena, although I have made a
booking on the boat that goes there six times a year. For
some months now I have been accumulating more and
more scattered pieces which all claim to belong to a jigsaw-
puzzle picture of this place I have never seen. St Helena is
becoming familiar to me, as a dream becomes familiar
when you look back at it and watch its sequences as they

repeat themselves on the screen of your waking mind. And when I have been there, then there will be two islands, the one that I have imagined and the one that I have seen, and although they will have some features in common, there will be others that have no point of connection or duplication.

The journey from England to St Helena takes sixteen days. There is a brief stop at the Canary Islands and then you travel on down between the continents of South America and Africa until you reach Ascension. I have been told that the men and women on this bleak island never appear together in public, and that if a stranger approaches they might scatter like sheep, or, if there is no means of escape, they avert their eyes and turn their backs and wait for the intrusion to pass them by. I have been told that at one end of the island there is a complex of corrugated-iron huts and hangars which serve as a base for the British Air Force on their way to and from the Falklands and at the other end of the island there is a town, which I imagine as a huddle of white-painted, square, low buildings, well suited to a shy people, but I might be wrong. I have seen only a couple of photographs of Ascension: one of them shows nothing more than the dark silhouette of a shape resting on calm water, with the sun shining out from behind a patch of clouds, while the other concentrates on a group of tombstones in the town cemetery, the names and dates of the people who died here in the eighteenth century carved into rough slabs of volcanic rock, and one of the stones has been decorated with the face of an angel, simple and frightened looking, with the features as dark holes dug into the round disc of the head and little wings sprouting out from where you would expect ears to grow.

Leaving Ascension I will travel for three days across an unknown sea, south and further south, with the strength of the Trade Winds blowing across the body of the ship. Finally I will catch sight of the steep cliffs of St Helena, a fortress of rock with the clouds always banked up above the mountains on the eastern side. As the ship approaches the land I will see the white buildings of the port of Jamestown crammed into a steep valley. I have been told that the high landscape behind Jamestown will make me think of north Wales, with sheep grazing on short grass among grey stone houses and grey stone boulders that have broken loose from the bare mountain ridges. But there are lemon and mango trees beside the grey houses, and geranium bushes as tall as trees with parakeets twittering among their branches, and spiders as big as tea cups, and the relentless croaking of little green frogs wherever there is a source of water. I will be going in the summer time, which will be winter there, and probably wet but not cold except on Deadwood Plain where Napoleon's house is situated. The people of the island speak with a soft lilting accent which makes them sound like Jamaicans who have lived for many years in Cornwall, or some other southern English county.

St Helena is ten and a half miles long and six miles wide, but it seems much bigger because it is so jagged and mountainous. It came into existence some sixty million years ago, towards the end of what is called the Tertiary Period, when the continents of the world split off from each other, and the earth's crust folded and buckled and molten rock erupted on to its outer surface. My young son has a book which illustrates this process on one large and colourful page. On the right-hand side prehistoric monsters are being hurtled to their death by a huge tidal wave, and on the left-hand side a rippling line of volcanoes is spitting out fire and brimstone. St Helena is part of such a volcanic chain which stretches from Tristan da Cunha in the south, up through Ascension, Cape Verde and the Canaries. Were it not for the Atlantic Ocean, these mountains would look similar to the Andes of South America, but as it is only their tips stick out above the water.

The coastline of St Helena is extraordinarily steep. From a distance it looks like a blank-walled fortress, but if the sunlight falls on the rock so that its structure and colour are revealed you can see it as a twisted folded curtain of purple and black and streaks of russet brown. The rim of the volcano's crater has become a semicircular ridge of mountains, and the erosion of rain and freshwater streams has sliced deep gorges into their sides. At the end of its eruptions the volcano threw up masses of soft basalts, and these were planted in the landscape in pinnacles and awkward towers in which the bubbling and bursting of the liquid rock can still be seen. A pale, grey-coloured column that looks like a huge shrouded figure goes by the name of Lot's Wife, and at a little distance along the same ridge of mountains can be seen the smaller giant figure of Lot himself. Other strange shapes have been given the name of Asses' Ears, the Turk's Cap, the Chimney, the Friar, and to the east, overhanging the sea, there is the mountain called the Barn, the profile of a man's head wearing a three-cornered hat, and looking, so they say, very much like Napoleon. During the years of his captivity the Emperor could gaze out of his bedroom window and see this vast reflection of himself, silhouetted against the sky.

For a long time, millions of years I suppose, St Helena was nothing more than a landscape of bare rock. Because it was so isolated, only certain forms of life could ever reach it and establish themselves here. The seeds of plants and trees could be carried on the waves or lodged in a broken branch and deposited somewhere along the coast, while the smallest seeds could be transported by the feet of sea birds. The eggs of certain insects, land snails and spiders could also have a chance of surviving a long and haphazard journey across the Atlantic. Slowly St Helena became colonised by vegetation, and a quantity of insignificant creatures without backbones. The island is so buffeted by wind and saturated by rain, that the temperature is never extreme; warm damp summers are followed by warm damp winters, making an atmosphere that is ideal for the growing of greenery. And so, in spite of the steepness of the rock, and the lack of any true soil, the seeds that found a place to root themselves flourished to an extraordinary degree, transforming St Helena into one entire forest. Trees fixed their roots into the steepest ravines, into the sheer faces of rock jutting out over the sea, and covered even the highest peaks of the mountains. There were gumwood, redwood and scrubwood trees, and he-cabbage palms, and she-cabbage palms, fern trees and umbrella trees, and many others that have never been given a Latin name or a botanical description. The most magnificent of all the trees were the black-hearted coromandel ebonies, that grew as slowly as oaks and stretched out their awkward rigid branches like vast candelabra. There were no grasses, but in the small clearings between the trees there were flowering shrubs and bushes; fat-leaved yellow samphire along the cliffs, wild celery and watercresses near the little streams and springs.

Feeding on the plants and the trees were at least one hundred and twenty-nine species of beetle. All of them but one were unique to this island, and most of them were small, dull-coloured members of the weevil family, with long hard noses well suited for tunnelling runways and nesting chambers under the bark of trees. There were also ten varieties of spiders that lived on beetles, and a number of large land snails that fed on leaves and stalks. At some stage in the island's early history a single species of bird made this place its home. It is a small, nervous, unremarkable, dapple-grey creature, related to the plover family and called the wirebird because of its long spindly legs.

Apart from the one bird, and the colonies of beetles, snails and spiders, the island was without inhabitants; a silent greenness, inaccessible and almost without sound or movement. But around its steep cliffs there was often intense activity. Seals, and the ungainly vegetarian sea cows, used to rest on the scattered rocks that were the remnants of the southern rim of the volcano's crater. The water was shallow here, and rich in many varieties of fish: congers and soldiers, old wives and bulls' eyes, and the rare coal fish. Turtles came to lay their eggs in the sands of the little bay that is now the port of Jamestown. Seabirds in their thousands nested on the cliffs, and a rock called Shore Island was so thickly covered with their white droppings that it could easily be mistaken for a ship in full sail.

Until the beginning of the sixteenth century, nobody knew of the existence of this little green island. But St Helena lies in the direct line of the south-east Trade Winds, and that meant that once the early navigators had rounded the Cape of Good Hope, and gained access to the South Atlantic, they were bound to come across it sooner or later. The Portuguese were the first. Admiral da Nova, in command of three warships, was returning to Portugal from India, and on 21 May 1502 he sighted a dark hump of land in an otherwise blank expanse of ocean. The date of this discovery was the birthday of Helena, the mother of the Emperor Constantine the Great, and that was how the island got its name.

Da Nova circled the island until he found a place, about the only place, where it was possible to anchor the boats and come ashore without scaling the cliffs. He and his sailors spent several days there. They explored the greenness of the great forests, and collected fresh water from the many springs. They caught quantities of fish that leapt up to swallow the shining bait of a bent nail tied to a piece of twine. They tasted the unsavoury flesh of the seabirds which sat in gregarious crowds and watched the sailors coming amongst them with clubs, making no attempt to fly away because they did not understand the danger they were in.

Before setting off on his journey, Da Nova ordered his

men to release a few goats. It was a usual thing to do at that time; a way of providing a source of fresh meat for any subsequent visitors who came here. The goats on St Helena had plenty of food and no predators and they soon multiplied and became very fat and large. When Captain Cavendish came to the island thirty years later he had never seen goats of such a size before, and thinking that they must be a native species he named them *caprus Hellenicus*. He wrote a description of the descendants of da Nova's original small band:

you shall see one or two hundred of them together, and sometimes you may behold them going in a flock almost a mile long. Some of them are as big as an ass, with a mane like a horse and a beard hanging down to the very ground. They will climb up the cliffs which are so steep that a man would think it a thing impossible for any living thing to go there.

We took and killed many of them for all their swiftness, for there be thousands upon the mountains. (Quoted in Gosse, p. 18)

CHAPTER III

Be not afeard. The isle is full of noises,
Sounds, and sweet airs, that give
delight, and hurt not.

Shakespeare, *The Tempest*

A place can be haunted by the people who knew it long ago and who stared at the stones under their feet, the leaves on the trees, and out at the far distances and horizons that encircled them. Something about St Helena's isolation seems to concentrate this sense of the land being haunted, soaked to the bone with the lives of people who were once here, and are now long since dead. It is as if the island's own loneliness creates a feeling of kinship that stretches back to everyone who has ever stood on this little platform which seems to be balanced on the very edge of the world.

I have been told that when the children of St Helena are asked who they consider to be central to their island's history, they do not think of mentioning Napoleon – he has become the property of historians and curious foreign visitors – but turn instead to the story of a Portuguese nobleman called Fernando Lopez. More than anyone else who has become embedded in this place, he stands out as the most vivid personality for them. Napoleon would have been told about Lopez as well; he was always glad to listen to the talk of slaves or children, people of no consequence who did not feel the need to be afraid of him, who would come and sit with him, and answer his questions. So he would have learnt all that there was to know about this strange exiled man, the island's first inhabitant, who seems to have been as lonely as the place he lived in. And since the two men had certain things in common, perhaps there were times later when their ghosts sat down together and discussed their thoughts about the life that they had led on the island.

After it had been discovered in 1502 St Helena remained uninhabited for several years. The wirebirds, snails and insects continued with their quiet existence, and the goats spread out across their new territory. Maybe the Portuguese stopped here occasionally to replenish their supplies of water and food as they made their slow journey back from the Indian subcontinent, but if they did, they never bothered to mention the fact in any of their surviving records, and no other nation as yet knew anything about the island's existence.

Fernando Lopez arrived here in 1515. Because of a crime he had committed he had no right hand, no left thumb, no nose and no ears, and the hair of his head, his eyebrows and his beard had been plucked out – a practice that was known as 'scaling the fish'. According to one account the fingers of his left hand had also been removed.

Lopez spent thirty years on the island. For most of that time he was entirely on his own, and for stretches of uninterrupted years he spoke to no one and was seen by no one, and went and hid in the greenness of the forest whenever a ship approached the harbour. On one occasion he did make a brief visit to Portugal, but then his only wish was to be allowed to return to his solitary home.

The story of this man with his grotesquely wounded face and his maimed hands is told by three early writers on Portuguese history. One of them saw him on the island, although it seems that he only caught sight of him from a distance and never managed to speak with him, and the other two wrote about him not long after his death. These accounts were written very simply, without comment or emotion, but just the idea of how this man must have looked serves to give him a complex personality, and it is easy to understand how the last years of his life were absorbed into the heart of the island, until man and place were in some ways indistinguishable.

Lopez was a Portuguese nobleman who left his home and his family and went with a group of soldiers under the leadership of General D'Alboquerque in search of new lands to conquer and claim for the Portuguese Empire. In 1510 they crossed the Indian Ocean from Arabia, and arrived in Goa on the south-west coast of India. After a brief battle they captured the ancient fortress town and claimed the ownership of the land that they stood on, and the vast unknown continent that lay beyond it. Because they had not got enough military strength to push their claim, D'Alboquerque set sail for Portugal to fetch more warships and more fighting men while Lopez and some of the soldiers were left behind to guard the fortress and to wait for the return of their general. D'Alboquerque was away for two years, and when he finally came back, bristling with reinforcements, he found that the men he had left behind had betrayed his trust in them, and had adopted the Muslim faith and the way of life of the local people. The traitors were rounded up without any resistance and brought before him, and since he had promised to be lenient they were not killed, although more than half of their number died during the three days that they were punished 'by black torturers and young men'. Lopez received the heaviest punishment because he was of noble birth and had been made responsible for the whole group. When it was all over, he and the others who had survived were released from the ropes and chains that bound them, and were set free to go wherever they chose. They all went and hid themselves somewhere in the countryside, so that neither their terrible wounds nor their shame could be seen.

Three years later D'Alboquerque was dead, and Lopez emerged out of hiding and took a passage on a ship bound for Portugal. He was planning to return to the wife and children he had not seen for so long, and to return to his house, his people, his language and his homeland. After many days at sea the ship stopped at the island of St Helena to replenish its supplies of water, and it was then that he realised he could not bring himself to complete his journey. He went ashore and hid himself deep in the forest. When the boat was ready to leave the sailors searched for him but could not find him, so they left some provisions on the shore and went on their way.

Lopez dug himself a hole in the ground in which to sleep. He had been provided with a barrel of biscuits and a few strips of dried meat, a tinder box and a saucepan. There were many edible herbs and fruits to be found, and it would not have been difficult for him to catch fish or nesting birds, or even one of the goats. The island was extremely benevolent; there were no wild animals here to harm him, no insects or reptiles to bite him, no diseases to sap his strength. In spite of the wind and the rain, the weather was always mild, and the trees were thick with sheltering leaves. A year went by before another ship appeared and dropped anchor in the bay that is now the port of Jamestown.

The crew was amazed when they saw the grotto and a straw bed on which he slept . . . and when they saw the clothing they agreed it must be a Portuguese man.

So they took in their water and did not meddle with anything, but left biscuits and cheeses and things to eat, and a letter telling him not to hide himself next time a ship came to the island, for no one would harm him.

Then the ship set off, and as she was spreading her sails a cockerel fell overboard, and the waves carried it to the shore and Fernando Lopez caught it and fed it with some rice which they had left behind for him. (Hakluyt Society, No. 62)

The cockerel was the first living creature to share the man's solitude. At night it roosted above his head and during the day it pattered after him and came to him when he called it. Time went on and Lopez learnt to be less afraid; slowly he grew into the habit of appearing when a ship was at anchor, coming to talk to the men who came ashore. Everyone who met him must have been moved by a sense of pity and of horror, and since Lopez refused to be separated from his island, the sailors treated him as if he was a sort of saint, a man carrying on his shoulders a huge weight of human suffering and estrangement. And since they could not take him with them and give him the freedom of their own way of life, they offered him gifts; they inundated him with anything they could find which they thought might please him. They gave him the seeds of vegetables and flowers; they gave him young palm trees and banana trees, pomegranates and lemons, oranges and limes. They also gave him living creatures: ducks and hens, pheasants and partridges, guinea fowl with their shrill warning shouts, peacocks with their harsh screams, turkeys, bullocks and cows, pigs, dogs and cats, even more goats, and, accidentally, a certain number of rats which came ashore when no one was looking. And so Lopez became a gardener and a keeper of livestock. With his single hand he worked tirelessly and relentlessly, planting and clearing, digging and tending, until under his care whole stretches of the landscape were utterly transformed. Among the ebony, the redwood and the gumwood trees he created gardens, vineyards and orchards, and because of the rain, the wind and the fertility of the soil, the seeds of many of the plants took root and flourished in parts of the island where he was not tending them, and because it was impossible to keep such a quantity of birds and animals in captivity, they also learnt to roam freely across the steep green landscape.

And this is how the island of St Helena became fused in people's minds with the idea of a rich garden growing on a rock in a distant ocean, a place of natural and yet unnatural perfection, fruitful throughout the year, cultivated and yet wild and without any human disturbances. It was hardly surprising that everyone who came here talked about this place that they had seen and the man who ruled over it like a king without subjects. In time the story was told to the king and queen of Portugal, and they summoned Lopez to appear before them at their royal palace in Lisbon. He came, unwillingly but obediently, and when he was offered anything he might desire, he asked simply to be taken to see the Pope in Rome so that he could confess his sins, and when he had seen the Pope, he begged permission to be taken back to the island he had come from. After this brief incursion into the world of men, Lopez was again visited by his old fears, and he stayed in hiding in the forest whenever he saw a ship approaching, and agreed to show himself only once it was promised in the king's name that no one would try a second time to carry him away.

And Fernando Lopez felt assured, so that he no longer used to hide himself, and spoke with those who came here, and gave them the produce of the island, which yielded in great abundance. And in the island he died, after living there a long time, which was in the year 1546. (Hakluyt Society, No. 62)

The extraordinary oasis that one man had created survived relatively unchanged for some years after his death. Portuguese sailors and soldiers who were too ill to continue on their journey would be left here to convalesce and gather their strength. A wooden chapel was built near the harbour, along with a few simple houses, but there were never more than a few men here at any one time, and there was no permanent settlement. The groves of citrus trees, the date palms and banana trees, the pineapples and pomegranates, all flourished, especially in the sheltered valley that rose up steeply from the harbour, and in a valley further to the east that came to be known as Lemon Valley. The wild domestic animals, the wild domestic birds and the rats ranged over the entire surface of the island, eating what they needed and multiplying. It was said that no matter what the season there was always enough fruit to fill the holds of six ships and there were wonderful herbs that could cure the scurvy within eight days. A man armed with a stick need not go far or exert himself much before he had secured the carcass of some plump bird or a large, well-fed and familiar animal.

On all sides the ancient forests stood as silent witnesses to the changes that were being brought about. The pigs, dogs, goats, cats and cattle were moving across the landscape like heavy earthbound locusts, but it would be a while before the effects of their presence were felt. The goats could eat the low branches and the young saplings of the trees, but they could not damage the bark of the old ebonies and gumwoods. The pigs could dig up the roots from the rich but shallow soil, but as long as the trees remained standing, that soil would be held fast, and no amount of rain or wind could sweep it away. So, in spite of the newly imported inhabitants, the island still had its strange and fertile beauty, with the old world and the new flourishing in apparent harmony.

The first book that attempted to provide a thorough and accurate account of St Helena was called the *General Description of Africa*. It was published in 1573, although the text seems to have been based on reports from travellers who visited the island during the 1550s. It explains that St Helena is an earthly paradise, a place where a man can refresh his soul as well as his body, where the climate is always mild, the food is plentiful, there is no sickness and not a single wild creature that could cause any harm. But by the time that the book was published, the island was already beginning to change character and its gentle benevolence was being shaken. Huge poisonous spiders, as big as a clenched fist, had arrived from Africa and settled in the banana trees, and there was a species of stinging fly the size of a grasshopper whose origins were unknown. Vicious battles were being fought between the colonies of dogs, cats and rats, and the rats were in the ascendancy and had taken to nesting in the high trees where they disrupted the roosting peacocks and other birds.

In 1581 the battle for mastery and power moved from the animal into the human realm. An English pirate captain called James Fenton came across St Helena accidentally, and determined to chase out the Portuguese so that he might possess the island and 'there be proclaimed Kyng'. This scheme came to nothing but in the following year another Englishman, Captain Cavendish, discovered the island while returning from a voyage round the world. He stayed there for twelve days, and he explored it, mapped it, wrote about it, and charted its position very exactly in the middle of the Atlantic Ocean. From then onwards the secret was broken, and a succession of ships from various countries arrived to examine the land and fight over its ownership. They developed the habit of collecting fruit by cutting down whole lemon trees and taking the trunk with its richly decorated branches on board ship with them when they were ready to leave. Sometimes they would uproot or trample on the produce of the wild gardens and orchards when they had no use for it themselves; it was a simple way of denying it to anyone who happened to arrive after them.

By 1610 only a few lemon trees were left and they were hard to find. There were none remaining on the hills close to the harbour, but there was still a grove big enough to provide 14,000 lemons at one picking at Lemon Valley, further along the coast. By 1634 it was said that there were less than forty lemon trees on the whole island: twenty in Lemon Valley and the rest scattered all over the place. However, the native trees were still growing thickly across most of the island's surface, and there was 'an abundance of Hoggs, store of little speckled guinea Henns, partridges and Pigeons, also doggs, and Catts (runne away) of whome the Companie killed divers'. (Gosse, pp. 29–30).

Maybe because it was so very far away and although many people had heard of it few had actually seen it, or maybe because human beings cannot bear very much reality and often prefer to see what they imagine rather than what lies before their eyes, whatever the reason, the written descriptions of St Helena were hardly altered in spite of the passage of time and the changes that time was bringing with it. By the late eighteenth century, when the island was almost naked, stripped of its covering of earth, plants and trees everywhere except in the higher regions and in cultivated gardens, the *Portable Geographer's Gazetteer*, a standard reference work which was available in a number of editions in French and in English, was able to explain confidently:

The hills are for the most part covered with verdure and large species of tree such as ebony etc. The valleys are very fertile in all kinds of excellent fruits, vegetables, etc. The fruit trees there bear at the same time flowers, green fruit and ripe fruit. The forests are full of orange, lemon and citrus trees. There are game birds in quantity, poultry and wild cattle. No savage or hurtful animal is found there, and the sea is full of fish. (Quoted in Masson, p. 98)

Napoleon had occasionally held St Helena in his mind, long before he made the slow sea crossing that brought him there from France. When he was a young man studying at the military academy at Auxonne he had filled a notebook with information about the lands that were at that time under British rule, and on the top line of an otherwise empty page he had written in his restless handwriting, 'St Helena, a small island'. In 1804 he even considered capturing this small island that could be so useful as a military base in the middle of the South Atlantic: '1,200 to 1,500 men will be required . . . The English are in no wise expecting this expedition and it will be a simple matter to surprise them' (Masson, p. 97). The expedition never materialised, but he did prepare himself by finding out all he could about the nature of St Helena. He was bound to have read the *Portable Geographer's Gazetteer* in its French edition, as well as the other descriptive books that were available at the time; they all echoed each other in their accounts of this green oasis where fruits were ripe all the year round. And so, when Napoleon was approaching the place that was to hold him captive for the final stage of his life, he had strong preconceptions about what it would be like.

CHAPTER IV

It is October and the year is 1989. The sky is white with smudges of grey cloud drifting across it. I have just come back from a walk over meadows and a ploughed field that is scattered with flints and pieces of chalk. You can often find fossils there, especially in a dip in the centre of the field where I suppose the sea once moved across a deep pool. Today I found a fragment of smooth yellow-coloured stone on which has been printed the mottled bumpy skin of some reptile, or perhaps a fish. I also found a rounded and unbroken lump of grey flint with the indentation of the staircase vertebra of two little tails pressed into it. One of the tails is twisted in a curl and looks as if it might suddenly flick itself into a new position: the other one is straight and somehow limp-looking in spite of being made of stone.

Beyond that field there is an area which was once an oak

wood; most of the trees were cut down a while ago, and now it is a straggling plantation of thin firs and even younger trees peering nervously out of their protective plastic tubes. Occasionally you come across a full-grown willow or poplar that was obviously not considered to be worth the effort of chopping down. The area is maintained for the sake of the pheasants that run through the rough grass and brambles like fleas in a dog's coat. When I was there just now I found two squirrels and five magpies strung by their necks on blue plastic twine and hanging from a fallen branch. I suppose it was felt by the owner of the land that they posed a threat to the financial returns of the pheasant industry.

It seems so very odd and yet it is so very common, to look at a stretch of landscape only in terms of the use it could be put to and the profit that could be extracted from it. To gaze at the precarious shifting whiteness of the Antarctic and to see in the mind's eye the pipes and pumps that can be made to suck oil from the heart of the rock; to be surrounded by an immense silence and to imagine hearing the somehow reassuring sound of machinery and human activity. I remember reading a journal written by an early settler in North America in which he said that the sound of great trees crashing to the ground and the smell of smoke as the woods were burnt to clear the land made the area feel less frightening to him and to other newly-arrived strangers like himself.

So much for the thoughts which briefly encircle me. The past leads into the present, and the island of St Helena is a witness to the changes it has seen and is still the same place, even though it has been put to many uses by the succession of people who have made claims to it and have adapted it to suit one purpose and then another. If you stare at the strangely naked landscape you can easily see what it must have lost, and you are close to knowing how it once was. Napoleon tried to make a garden that would give him some privacy and some shade on a desolate plain where nothing grew; the same place where Fernando Lopez hid himself in greenness.

When it was first drawn on to the map of the world, the little island of St Helena was considered to be valuable simply because of its position on the trade route from the East Indies and the Cape, and because it was able to supply passing ships with much needed provisions of water and fresh meat, fruit and vegetables. But very soon people became curious to know in what way the island could be found valuable in itself. Was there some precious mineral, gold perhaps, or copper or tin, wedged between the layers of folded volcanic rock? Was the soil suitable for growing coffee beans or indigo? Could sea salt be collected in basins where the waves were thrown up on the flat cliffs above Prosperous Bay? What was the market price for the droppings of the seabirds which coated Shore Island with such a brilliant whiteness? How many of those ancient and ponderous sea cows could be found browsing on seaweed in the shallow waters, and how many kegs of good oil, suitable for lamp-burning, could be extracted from one sea cow? And given that a single, healthy black slave working on a plantation could be expected to support four white men, how many yam plants were needed to feed fifty slaves for a single year?

In 1651 the island became what was known at that time as a factory. It was no longer to be seen as a port of call for passing ships, but as a trading depot, owned and operated by a consortium of English businessmen known as the East India Company. A governor and a group of officials were established on the island and were in charge of operating the factory, but all important decisions had to be made by a board of directors who sat in Company headquarters in London. None of the directors had ever seen St Helena, and so when they needed to answer an urgent request it was often difficult for them to understand the exact nature of the problem. On top of that it took at least half a year, and sometimes much longer, for a communication to travel to England and back again. The Company was answerable to no one except its shareholders, and it had one single and simple aim: to make a profit.

And so it was that everything pertaining to St Helena – its rocks, its trees, its soil, the birds that flew above it and the sea creatures that swam around it, as well as the people and animals who had recently adopted it as their new home – was seen in terms of the money that it could be expected to make for the Company or which the Company hoped to make from it. In the words of the contract of ownership drawn up by King Charles II in 1673:

> We have given, granted, and confirmed, to the Governor and Company and their Successors, St Helena, with all rights, profits, territories, and appurtenances . . . and all soyles, land, fields, woods, mountains, farms, lakes, pools, harbours, rivers, bays, isles, islets . . . with the fishing of all sorts of fish . . . and all the veins, mines, quarries, as well as royal mines, whether the same be already discovered or not discovered . . . and all royalties, revenues, rents, privileges, franchises, immunities . . . (Brooke, pp. 325–6)

During those early years the governor of the island was responsible for some seventy men and women from England and two dozen black slaves from Madagascar. The English settlers were men and women who had no money and no possessions and it was simple desperation that persuaded them to set out across the sea to a place they knew nothing about, with only the vague hope that life in another land might be easier. They were told that St Helena was a garden paradise, and they were also told that each man who came there would be given twenty acres of land, two cows, seeds and plants, breeding stock, slave labour, and enough biscuits, salt beef and oil to last him and his family for the first nine months of residency. A settler who chose to live on the eastern side of the island facing the relentless Trade Winds, was offered a double portion of land as an extra bonus, but once people had seen that side they mostly preferred to avoid it. Although a few of the settlers managed to grow rich, the majority remained very poor, and their position was little more than that of tenant farmers. One woman received thirty lashes on her naked body because she scandalised a ship's captain, and another had to pay a fine of one shilling because she cursed the island on a Sunday. The prison and the lash were in regular use, with the slaves below the settlers and the settlers below the Company officials, and if a man failed to work hard enough on his own land then that land was confiscated and he was returned to England empty-handed.

Over the following years the regulations and restrictions which governed the island's human inhabitants multiplied and mutated into rules that seemed to have no purpose at all, and there was scarcely any aspect of daily life that did not need to have permission granted and payment made. A man wishing to slaughter his own pig needed to buy a licence to do so, and to apply for a second licence if he wanted to sell some of the meat to his neighbour. It was forbidden to gather the edible leaves of the samphire bushes that grew along the cliffs because the Company's partridges were thought to use this plant in their nest building. All seabirds belonged to the Company, but for a fee a settler could obtain permission to collect their eggs from Thursday to Saturday during the months of October and November. All land that was not under cultivation, however barren or inaccessible it might be, formed part of the Company's Wastes, and it was a trespass to walk on it and a crime to shoot a bird or a wild goat on it. The Company's record books are filled with the fines and punishments that were imposed on the settlers and the slaves, the uprisings that were put down, the criminals and rebels who were hanged or imprisoned, or made to suffer some inventive form of torture.

From the very beginning of St Helena's history as a commercial venture a sense of tragedy and despair seems to cling to everything. Although there were many speculations about the great riches that could one day be made, the island proved stubbornly unrewarding. One man thought he had found gold and everyone was ordered to dig like rabbits in search of more, but it turned out that what had been discovered was only iron pyrites or fool's gold. Further excavations revealed nothing more interesting than some patches of limestone that could be burnt and turned into building lime, and a dense claylike substance which bore the unlikely name of Puzzolana and proved very useful in mending leaking roofs and making simple watercourses.

Coffee beans, sugar cane and indigo all were planted and tended and watched over, but none of them flourished. Beans, carrots, barley and potatoes did quite well, but the plant that was most responsive to the climate and the soil was the watery yam. Young yams were imported from Madagascar in the same ships that were bringing new slaves, and when the factory was at the height of its production in the late eighteenth century a thousand yams a day were being fed to the 'Company's Blacks, Piggs and Fowls'.

In spite of the fact that none of the plantations were financially successful, the Company pushed on with the work of clearing the land of trees to make way for more regulated lines of crops and more open pastures to feed lean cattle and wild goats. At first they concentrated on the western side which was best suited for cultivation, but eventually they turned their attention to the east. This area was wetter and colder and more misty than anywhere else on the island, and the constant battering of the Trade Winds made people feel that they were going mad. It was a wide plain that swept down towards the cliffs along the coast, and it was known as the Great Wood because it was covered with a vast and silent army of ebony and redwood trees. Some of these trees were used for fuel or as building material, but it was the tanning industry that caused their ruin. The settlers used to tan the hides of their goats and cattle using acids imported from England, but then in the late 1600s it was discovered that if the bark of redwood and ebony was boiled in water it produced a liquid that was just as powerful as the acid, and much cheaper.

It would have been possible to strip the bark from the branches of the trees and then to leave them for several years to recover and mend their skins, but people were impatient and just as before they had cut down the lemon trees in order to collect the fruit, so now they stripped whole trunks from root to crown, and left the naked trees to die. The governor of the island took note of the fact that the Great Wood was growing smaller and smaller, but feeling that he could not stop the tanners from tanning he decided to put the dead trees to use:

> The Redwood and Ebony trees are most of them destroyed by the Tanners . . . we find that Ebony wood will burn lime and being informed that there is a huge quantity of that wood which lies dead on hills near Sandy Bay, the Governor and Captain Mashborne went to view it. (Janisch, p. 90)

Over the following years it became apparent that the eastern side of the island was changing character. The young trees that grew up from scattered seeds were quickly destroyed by the goats and pigs before they could reach maturity, and the wind and rains were steadily tearing at the thin covering of soil. In 1709 the governor wrote a letter to the Company in London, saying that the island was being ruined by the loss of its trees and was suffering from terrible and unprecedented floods and droughts. He asked permission to get rid of the wild goats as soon as possible, in order to try to save the young trees that were still left in Great Wood. The reply when it finally arrived was brief and uncompromising. The Company had considered the problem and had decided that 'The goats are not to be destroyed, being more valuable than the ebony.' (Wallace, p. 296)

So that was it. The goats and the pigs stayed, the tanners went on tanning, there was plenty of wood available for burning and for building, and bit by bit the island lost its outer shell:

Such vast floods of water descended from the middle of the island as did abundance of damage, and carried away the soil in an incredible manner, with both grass and trees, yams and stone walls before it . . . The fine earth being washed away in such a great quantity that the sea for a great way round the island looked like black mudd. (Janisch, p. 170)

This process continued throughout the eighteenth century, until the eastern side of the island had been turned into a barren plain where nothing grew except for a few straggling gumwood trees which provided no shade and were not even good food for goats. In some places the broken stumps and trunks of the ebony wood could be seen lying like black boulders on the ground, and the wood was so hard that it survived generations of wind and rain without rotting. This was why the area that had been known as Great Wood took on a new name, and was now called Deadwood, and everyone who went there remarked on the sadness of the landscape and the way that even the climate here seemed to have become unnatural:

An alteration of weather often happens in less than an hour's space, from sultry heat to very cold, and the mountainy parts are not only windy, but are always exposed to great damps and fogs, even in the times we call the dry season. (Janisch, p. 33)

It soon became apparent to the East India Company and their various official representatives that St Helena had lost the few assets it once possessed and seemed to offer no new commercial possibilities which could be explored. Most of the trees had gone except in the highest regions, the rock was only rock, and the earth, what was left of it, was only earth. The herds of goats, cattle and pigs had learnt to adapt to life here by becoming very lean and wild, while the inhabitants were poor and often hungry and troubled by the presence of rats, fleas, and cockroaches in their houses, mice and insects in their fields. The one and only constant and reliable source of income was the regular arrival of ships travelling back from the Cape and the East Indies with crew and passengers on board who tended to be hungry and tired and in need of entertainment and strong drink. Hundreds of ships arrived at Jamestown harbour each year, and the islanders soon realised that it was more profitable to give up all attempts at being farmers and to take up instead the profession of shopkeepers, innkeepers and brothel-keepers.

By the end of the eighteenth century the port of Jamestown had a single main street that was dense with cafés and 'inferior habitations'. The buildings were all painted with whitewash which dazzled the eye in the sun, and the one main street and the little side streets were 'strewn with drunkards, while the Hospital overflowed with patients'. The islanders produced a powerful local rum and 40,000 gallons of this mixture were being consumed each year. There were always thirty or forty ships at anchor in the harbour, and with each new arrival a small crowd of men and women would gather at the quay to examine the faces of those who came ashore and to prepare to answer their particular needs. The island was known as the ocean roadhouse, or less politely, as the Atlantic brothel.

Lands that had once been cleared and cultivated were either left under the supervision of a few slaves or were deserted altogether. Fruit trees were uncared for and even lemon juice had to be imported. The fresh food that did grow on the island was sold at fantastically high prices, and the few farmers who produced enough to be able to provide the shops in Jamestown ran a monopoly and preferred to let their fruit and vegetables lie rotting on the ground and their meat go putrid rather than submit to a drop in their prices.

Anything that was not grown on the island had to be imported by the Company, and they had their own system of taxation and import duties which no one could argue with. Strangers who spent a few days while their ship replenished its supplies were shocked by the amount of money that was taken from them and the little that they received in return:

> Treading the fields and streets and seeing a new people, wandering over rocks and imbibing the odour of the fresh earth was all that most could afford . . .
>
> He who desires a fresh meal, should first reflect on the extravagance he is going to commit. He dare not taste a mutton chop if indeed such a thing can be had, under a guinea. Killing a sheep is an event of almost as much consequence as Bonaparte annihilating an Austrian or Prussian army in Europe, and the slaughter of a bullock is nearly equal to the subjugation of a kingdom. (Prior, p. 85)

Then on 12 October 1815 a boat arrived at Jamestown bearing important news. Napoleon had been defeated at

Waterloo three months previously. Rather than attempting to escape from his enemies he had decided to trust in the generosity and hospitality of English law and had surrendered himself to the British Government. He had apparently expected to be lodged in a 'fairly large' country house not too far from London but instead, and much to his dismay, he was being brought to St Helena as a prisoner-of-war who should be 'restrained in his personal liberty to whatever extent may be necessary'. He had been allowed to select: 'three officers, who, together with his surgeon, will be permitted to accompany him to St Helena. Twelve domestics including the servants of the officers, will also be allowed. It must be distinctly understood that all those individuals will be liable to restraint during their attendance upon him and their residence at St Helena, and they will not be permitted to withdraw from thence without the sanction of the British government' (letter read out to Napoleon by Sir Henry Bunbury quoted in Aubry, p. 90).

Napoleon, or as he was now officially described, General Bonaparte, was due to arrive in four days' time. The immediate effect of this extraordinary piece of information was, 'a sudden and enormous rise in prices. Eggs which were before about three shillings a dozen, now advanced to a shilling a piece. Almost every other article of produce rose in the same proportion and even land itself assumed an increased value of forty percent.' (*Morning Chronicle*, 9 Dec. 1815)

But it was not only the cost of living that Napoleon affected so dramatically. The ship that carried him here also carried a message explaining that St Helena no longer belonged to the East India Company. It was now the property of the British Government, and it must cease to function as a factory and learn to function as a prison. Once Napoleon had been brought ashore he was to be swallowed into the belly of the island and then everything was to be closed off and turned inwards, concentrating on him and holding him tightly fixed in one place. There was always the possibility that someone might try to rescue him, prise him off the rock and carry him away, but this threat was never so vivid as the idea of the danger contained in the man himself.

Suddenly new laws and restrictions sprang up in all directions. From now until further notice, no ship could approach the harbour of Jamestown without official permission, even if they were in desperate need of water. And if for some special reason a ship was allowed to drop anchor, then no passenger or crew member could come ashore without producing a document signed by the governor of the island and explaining exactly where they wanted to go and who they wished to visit. Local fishermen could only go out in their boats at certain hours of the day and they needed to carry a dated licence with them at all times. A curfew was imposed on the inhabitants, and anyone found wandering out of doors after nine o'clock at night and without a legal pass was liable to be arrested. A place with a population of some 3,500 individuals was inundated by wave upon wave of strangers who had come to stay for an indefinite period of time. Some two thousand soldiers were imported from England and a further five hundred naval personnel were at anchor in a flotilla of warships that bobbed and rocked in the water a little distance from the harbour. There were also government officials, wives and children, servants, secretaries and assistants, and they were all in need of accommodation and food and some sort of activity to keep them busy in body and mind. Every one of them was aware of the presence of Napoleon, although few would ever have an opportunity of catching sight of him, let alone speaking with him. He was there somewhere at the centre of the crowd, like a queen bee surrounded by the moving intensity of her hive, or perhaps more accurately, like some small creature that has been covered by an army of ants.

CHAPTER V

My black servant took me a long walk
over the rocks and hills until we
reached a garden where we saw a man
sitting.
'That is he!' said the black man, 'that
is Bonaparte! He eats three sheep a day
and all the little children he can lay
hands on!'

Thackeray, *Roundabout Papers*

It is not easy to stare at a person who is aware of being
stared at. You see yourself reflected in an answering gaze
and thoughts get in the way, distracting the process of
looking. Perhaps only children, tyrants, savages and the
clinically insane can presume on the freedom of staring
intensely and carefully, allowing the eyes to move and rest
and move again until they are satisfied that they have seen
all that they wish to see.

When she was four years old my daughter made friends
with a rather grand lady who was on the edge of being a
hundred. She would clamber up on to the double bed with
its white counterpane and sit there close to the delicate
contours of the woman's legs, chattering and asking
questions, undisturbed by the long silences and incon-
sequential answers she received. As she talked and lis-

tened she examined the old lady minutely. She stared unsmiling into the distant eyes that were deep and hooded like the eyes of certain birds of prey. She stroked the long hair, the lace of a nightdress, and picked up the pale hands with their delicate tracery of lines and veins, the nail of each finger meticulously painted a vivid red. The old woman seemed to enjoy this scrutiny and when her hands were being held and turned she looked at them with a slightly surprised expression, as if she was wondering what they were and what use they could be put to.

Whenever a ship approaches the island of St Helena a crowd gathers on the quay, waiting to see the new strangers who are being brought to them. They watch the passengers make the awkward descent into a little boat that will carry them on the final stage of their journey, and they watch how each individual manages to negotiate the step that has to be taken from the wobbling and heaving boat on to the rock and concrete of dry land. They move closer to get a better look at faces, bodies, luggage, and they maintain a silence of concentration that can seem hostile to anyone who is not used to being dealt with in this way. Often a nickname settles on a visitor from this very first impression, so that a woman who trips and blushes in her confusion becomes Mrs Redface and a man who behaves impatiently becomes Old Damnyou. Napoleon, walking through the silent crowd that came to witness his arrival, said that he felt like a wild beast, caged but still dangerous and set among a people who had never encountered such a creature before.

The ship that carried him to St Helena came in sight of land on the evening of 14 October 1815. He went out on deck as soon as he heard that his destination had been reached, and just before the sudden darkness of a tropical night he was able to catch a brief glimpse of a mass of rock surrounded by calm black waters. The next morning he rose early and stood in the bows of the ship to examine the island with his field-glasses. He was shocked to realise that it looked even more inhospitable by day than it had done by night. He could not see much beyond the cramped white houses of Jamestown and the steep cliffs that guarded them, but what he could see must have appeared like the dream of a military strategist who feared attack from all sides. The island was very well defended. In the words of one visitor who had been here during the previous year, it seemed to have been turned into a 'vast depot for the instruments of war'. A roar of cannon shot had announced Napoleon's arrival the night before, and now he could see the noses of cannons bristling from the cliffs. Watchtowers and sentry boxes and the jagged outline of a telegraphic relay system could be discerned against the skyline, and everywhere there was the fluttering of the Union Jack and the glint of polished metal as the soldiers moved this way and that, making the necessary preparations to receive their prisoner. Napoleon turned to the man who was standing next to him and remarked drily, 'It is not a pretty place to live. I would have done better to stay in Egypt' (Gourgaud, vol. I. p. 66). Then without further comment he retired to his cabin.

During the course of that day the English admiral who was the captain of the ship, the governor of the island, an English doctor and a St Helenian shopkeeper, all came to see Napoleon in his cabin and to talk to him about the plans for his immediate future. He questioned the governor about the cost of living on this strange place, and what the climate was like; how many soldiers were already stationed here and how many more were expected. He asked the doctor about the birth rate, the death rate and the most common causes of sickness and mortality among the islanders. He asked the admiral when he was going to be allowed to leave the ship and where he was going to live, and he asked the shopkeeper if he would be so kind as to mend two gold watches which had both stopped working during the long sea voyage.

On the following morning the admiral went ashore with the governor to take a look at the island and to inspect the house that had been chosen as the future home of 'Napoleon and his suite'. He came back later that day filled with rather muted enthusiasm for a 'pleasant residence' called Longwood, situated on the eastern side of the island in an area that was known as Deadwood. He said that the house still needed to have certain essential repairs and alterations made before it was ready, and he suggested that Napoleon and his servants and companions, a total of twenty-six men, women and children, might like to stay at a boarding house in Jamestown. Indeed they could make their way there immediately.

Ever since Napoleon's ship and its five accompanying vessels with their load of soldiers and supplies had dropped anchor in the bay, the people of St Helena had been anxious to catch sight of the prisoner. Some of them were familiar with his name and with the life that he had led before coming here, but to others he was nothing more than a floating and evocative sound, like 'England', 'snow' or 'battlefield', that hinted at things that could not be clearly imagined. Nevertheless it was obvious to everyone that this man was very important, and even now his presence was stirring like a rumour across the island. When Napoleon trained his field-glasses on the quay he could see a large crowd gathered at the water's edge and many more people moving aimlessly among the houses. He asked if he could go ashore at night to avoid being stared at too closely, and the admiral agreed to delay the landing until just before it was dark. And so at six o'clock on the evening of 17 October, a little boat carried Napoleon to the island.

It is said that the whole population of St Helena, some three and a half thousand people, had made its way into

Jamestown and was waiting for him there. When they realised that he was coming ashore under the cloak of darkness they lit flaming torches so that they could see him more clearly. The governor and a guard of armed sentries were ready to receive him, and a double line of armed soldiers had made a narrow path that led to the boarding house. Behind these uniformed men there stood a closely packed crowd of slaves and settlers, men, women and children, blacks and whites and 'free people of colour', their faces flickering in the light of the flames.

Napoleon walked between the English admiral who had been responsible for bringing him here, and a French general who had come with him in his exile. He was wearing his black hat that made him look taller than he really was and a black coat that made him look larger. As he moved a diamond star that was pinned to the satin band of the Legion of Honour tied across his chest, glinted in the torchlight. The pressure of the crowd became so great that it was with difficulty that he and his companions could move forward at all, and the soldiers were ordered to turn and face the people with fixed bayonets, and to guard the side roads to stop anyone from blocking the way ahead of them.

The boarding house of Mr Porteous stood on one side of Jamestown's single main street. It was a square white building with three windows on the ground floor and five windows on the first floor and narrow steps with a little iron railing leading to the front door. Napoleon was shown to a room on the first floor in which there was a single bed and a window looking out into the street and a small public garden where geraniums and palm trees had been planted in symmetrical order around a few benches and a gravel path. The crowd gathered in the street and in the park, talking softly now, singing, calling Napoleon by name, waiting for the excitement to pass and let them go home.

Napoleon lay down on his bed and his two servants, Marchand and St Denis, stretched themselves out like dogs across the doorway. When the house was quiet again, the cockroaches and the bedbugs, the rats and the fleas could return to their night-time activities.

On the morning of the following day Napoleon was up and dressed very early and by six o'clock he was ready to set out for Longwood. The admiral had arranged to meet him at this hour, so that they could begin their ride before the sun became too oppressive, and when he arrived he brought with him a small black stallion whose name, so they say, was Hope. And so Napoleon, dressed now in the bright green satin costume of a Chasseur du Gard and glistening with medals and decorations, mounted on a black horse called Hope, set off with the English admiral, the French general and the two French servants, up the winding track that led out of Jamestown and into the landscape beyond it. He never again entered the streets of Jamestown, but Mr Porteous was quick to realise the commercial possibilities of what had taken place in his boarding house. He cut out the entry in the visitors' book that registered the names of the guests who had stayed that one night, and had it mounted in a frame; afterwards anyone who was interested in history and human destiny could arrange to sleep in the Emperor's Room.

Meanwhile Napoleon and his companions continued on their way. It would have taken them an hour and a half to reach the top of the road which led out of Jamestown, and there before them lay their first view of the island itself. To the west they could see trees and houses and cultivated fields and in the distance the governor's residence: a solid-looking mansion with its walls painted dove grey, its shutters painted white and a wide curving drive leading to it which passed lawns and flower beds and stately trees. To the east the land became increasingly bleak and mountainous, with the black volcanic rock hardly hidden by the thin soil and nothing much growing except pale cactuses and geranium bushes and no movement of birds or creatures. They went this way, following a track that led them up and up until they reached a narrow gorge, Hutt's Gate, standing like a tall open doorway leading into the plateau of Deadwood. Now to their left they could see a steep ravine of rock and twisted trees and at the heart of it a sudden greenness where a spring bubbled out over the earth. At that time this place was still known as Geranium Valley, although later it would be called the Valley of the Tomb when Napoleon lay there with an iron railing protecting the slab of stone that marked his grave and the earth trampled by the feet of the people who had come to see him here. Past Geranium Valley they needed to dismount and lead their horses through a strange dip in the landscape known as the Devil's Punchbowl, and then up on the other side they were back on the plain once more where nothing grew but straggling gumwood trees.

Near to the coast the antlike figures of soldiers and slaves and donkeys were busy carrying the goods and provisions that were needed for the new military camp of Deadwood where some two thousand men would have the task of watching Napoleon. Straight ahead they could see the simple outline of a low building painted yellow and roofed in grey slate, with a few sheep and a single tall tree to keep it company. This was Longwood House, Napoleon's future residence.

Longwood had been built fifty years previously by one of the governors of the island as a cattle barn and storage shed. He had looked at Deadwood plain and thought that perhaps if a wall was made to keep the goats out, then a new generation of trees could be persuaded to grow here, or wheat could be cultivated or a fine herd of Madagascan cattle could be raised. So he started to organise the building of a high wall that would contain two square miles of land,

and he arranged for Longwood to be erected ready to store the first harvest of wheat and to provide shelter for the cattle during the seasons when the weather was too wet and cold for them out on the plain. However, during the same year that the building was finished and the three subsequent years, there was a severe drought which meant that the wheat never ripened, the sapling trees all died and the Madagascan cattle did not grow fat. The wall was only partially completed so that it kept nothing in and nothing out and only added to the feeling of desolation that hung over the place. Longwood was left empty and unused with its one tree that drew lines of shadow across it for a few hours on sunny days, and no source of water or shelter from the wind.

The original building was a row of four low rooms that led directly into each other and several small annexes that were to be used for storing extra machinery or cattle in need of special attention. The rafters were exposed and the floor was bare earth. It was left untouched for a number of years, until in 1812 a deputy governor called Mr Skelton decided to turn it into a summer residence where he and his family could spend a few weeks every year. He arranged for floorboards to be laid above the earth and dried cattle dung, and he had the roof repaired and tarred and low ceilings fitted. A drawing-room was added to the front of the house, the walls were washed and papered, and then the place served its new purpose quite adequately.

Napoleon and the admiral, the general and the two servants arrived at Longwood. Mr Skelton and his wife had met the admiral on the previous day and they were now waiting to welcome their guests and to serve them luncheon. The weather was mild, although a wind was blowing and the meeting was brief, formal and courteous. The little party left at three o'clock and began to make its slow way back to Jamestown. Napoleon told his servant

Marchand that he was only 'moderately charmed' by the house, which seemed to be a place 'conducive to mildew in furniture and rheumatism in people'. He was disconcerted by the fact that it possessed neither shade nor water and was exposed to the prevailing south-east wind.

Once they had again passed through Hutt's Gate and were making their way down the mountainside, Napoleon saw far below them a low white building set in a very green garden, and he watched it as it grew closer. The family who lived there were at the same time standing on the lawn of their garden studying the slow progress of the five horsemen.

> Following the windings of the road they now gleamed in the sun's rays and were thrown into brilliant relief by the dark background behind, and then disappearing we gazed earnestly until from some turn in the road they flashed again upon us. Sometimes we saw a single white plume, or the glitter of a weapon in the sun. To my already excited fancy, it suggested the idea of an enormous serpent with burnished scales, occasionally showing himself as he crawled to our little abode. (Mrs Abell, p. 17)

This house was known as The Briars and it was occupied by Mr and Mrs Balcombe and their four children. Mr Balcombe had worked for the East India Company as the purveyor of goods on the island and he was a genial man with a large belly and a fondness for wine and conversation; his wife was said to look very much like the Empress Josephine. He had two sons who were then four and five years old, and two daughters, Betsy and Jane, who were thirteen and fifteen. The whole family had been part of the crowd of spectators in Jamestown on the previous day and now as they watched Napoleon for a second time they saw him and his companions pause for a moment and then make their way along the row of pomegranates and banyan trees that led to the house. They reached the garden gate and the admiral, the general and the two servants dismounted, but Napoleon stayed on horseback, and as he led the way across the lawn his horse's hoofs cut deep marks into the grass.

The unexpected guests were welcomed by the Balcombes, and offered seats in the garden and refreshments. The thirteen-year-old Betsy was the only member of the family who could speak French fluently and since Napoleon had hardly any words of English she took on the role of intermediary. Napoleon looked intently at the house and the garden and the people and then he asked if he might be able to live here until Longwood had been made ready for him. Mr Balcombe did not hesitate in saying that he could and messengers were at once sent to Jamestown to arrange for a few essential items to be brought to him that evening. The admiral and the general departed with the messengers while Napoleon, his two servants and his hosts went into the parlour. There he talked and sang and stalked around the room as if he was alone and the place belonged to him, staring at the people and the objects around him and laughing his barking laugh. Many years later Betsy Balcombe wrote a book in which she tried to describe her impressions of this guest who came to live in her family home. It is clear from what she says that, unlike most people who met Napoleon, she was not frightened of him, and although she was curious about his past life she was not particularly impressed by it. She admired his medals and decorations as if they were the plumage of some rare bird. She watched the way his eyes seemed to change colour from blue to grey to brown. She felt his hair which was as soft as the hair of a young child, and she wondered why his teeth were so dark until she realised that it came from eating so much liquorice. She took his hands in her own to examine them. Usually it is only very old people who will accept such scrutiny, but Napoleon on St Helena was in many ways already an old man, with an old man's detached curiosity.

I try to see him there in a house that has long ceased to exist, on a distant island that I have not yet visited. I know the green jacket and waistcoat he is wearing because it hangs on a tailor's dummy in a glass case in a museum in Paris. The cloth is worn but it is still a very sharp bright green like young grass, and the whole torso is surprisingly delicate. In that same museum you can see the white britches he would have worn, pinned to a wall like the skin taken from an animal. His boots are there as well, small and very shiny, and in the case next to the clothes there is a glass dome in which lies a plaster cast of his right hand, the thumb across the palm, the fingers small and rounded. Near to the hand there is a plaster cast of the face as it was in death, but it is so quiet, white and still that it is difficult to imagine it as ever having belonged to a person. Hair, hand, jacket, teeth; I try to see Napoleon in the front parlour of a house belonging to an English merchant, the family sitting around him, formal and yet eager to please, confused by the importance and the oddness of the occasion. Crowded into this little room, their futures lie before them and I can see what will happen to each one of them after this day, after the years that are still to come.

Napoleon questions Betsy about her studies, her life here on the island, and most particularly about her knowledge of geography.

'What is the capital of France?'
'Paris.'
'Of Italy?'
'Rome.'
'Of Russia?'
'Petersburg now, Moscow formerly.'
On my saying this he turned abruptly around, and

fixing his piercing gaze full on my face, demanded sternly, 'Who was it who burnt it to the ground?'

He repeated the question and I stammered, 'I do not know sir.'

'Yes yes,' he replied, laughing violently. 'You know very well. It was I who did it. I burnt it to the ground!'

On seeing him laugh I gained a little courage and said, 'I believe sir the Russians burnt it, to get rid of the French.'

He again laughed and seemed pleased to find that I knew anything about the matter. (Mrs Abell, p. 24)

CHAPTER VI

'What do you suppose is the use of a
child without any meaning? Even a
joke should have some meaning – and
a child's more important than a joke, I
hope.'

Lewis Carroll, *Through the Looking Glass*

When Napoleon told the Balcombes that he would like to
stay here in their house until his own living quarters at
Longwood had been made ready for him, they at once
offered to move to Jamestown so that he and the twenty-six
people who had come with him from France could make
use of all the rooms at The Briars. But no, he said he would
be quite happy to live in the garden, in a little white-
painted building made of glass and wood and wrought
iron known as the Pavilion. Originally it had been intended
as a ballroom, but now it served occasionally as a guest
room, or as a dining-room. It was twenty feet long and
fourteen feet wide, with six tall windows and two high
doors, and a floor of shining, polished rosewood that had
been imported from England. The room was at present
empty of furniture, and that must have emphasised the

bones of the building, carefully made in the Adams style, with a lot of fluting and cornicing and carved fretwork that gave the painted wood and metal the appearance of sculpted icing sugar. A narrow staircase, as steep as a ladder, led to a loft divided into two rooms, and each one was just large enough to hold a single mattress. The Pavilion stood on the lawn, not many yards from the Balcombes' house, close to a walled garden of fruit trees and vegetables, and a sheltered grape arbour where a table and chairs were set out. Chickens, donkeys and cows could be heard throughout the day, along with the occasional screech of a peacock.

Napoleon's request was at once obeyed. The Balcombes offered him any items of furniture that he might wish to use, and arranged for curtains to be made to fit the Pavilion's bare windows. On the first day he had asked for certain things that he considered immediately essential to be brought to him from Jamestown, and over the following weeks a steady stream of possessions were accumulated around him. Many people display their power and their personal history in the shape of the goods that they own and wish to have seen. A Trobriand Island chieftan sits beside a pile of taro roots, a lady of the court wears fine jewels, a warrior might collect skulls. One by one Napoleon summoned the symbols of his past to him, and one by one they were brought here by donkeys, slaves and soldiers. But when the contents of the crates and boxes were unpacked and set out, they did not transform the Pavilion into a palace, but into something that was partly a museum and partly a stage set waiting for the play to begin again. And Napoleon himself, standing in the centre of these costly souvenirs, did not seem to be their rightful owner, but rather an official guard who had been ordered to watch over them.

Miniature portraits of the Imperial family – wife, child, first wife, mother – were hung on the Pavilion's white walls, gazing out from frames encrusted with jewels, just as they had gazed out from the pale muslin sides of a tent on the field of battle, or from the gold-leaf and eggshell-blue setting of a bedroom in the Tuileries in Paris.

He chose to sleep on a narrow metal campbed that had been with him on so many military campaigns, and it was hung with bright green taffeta silk curtains that made it look like a child's cot from a book of nursery rhymes. He had also brought with him a silver travelling case containing a set of toilet articles and an exquisite washstand and basin; a silver bowl supported by the outstretched wings of golden swans.

One writer insists that Napoleon's tin bath was brought to the Pavilion and that later, when he got a better one at Longwood, it was turned into a sunken fish pond in his garden, but this seems unlikely since no one mentions the Emperor taking a bath while he was a guest of the Balcombes, although every other habit of his daily life is carefully described. It is, however, certain that he had with him here the box containing his collection of decorated snuff-boxes, and on one occasion he decided to fill in a blank space of time by setting them all out before him like glistening toys, and saying, 'Now, let me make an inventory of all my wealth!' He showed the snuff-boxes to the Balcombe children, explaining that this one had belonged to the Tsar of Russia and that one with the pearls to Louis XII and this one bordered with diamonds was a portrait of himself at his coronation in 1804.

Napoleon was especially proud of a set of Sèvres china that had been presented to him by the people of Paris. Each cup, bowl, dish and plate was a detailed illustration of some event in his life, and he boasted that they were worth at least twenty-five napoleons a piece. There he was crossing the Alps with his long hair blown by an icy wind; there he was fighting bravely at the battle of Marengo, at the battle of Leipzig, standing among the dead and the dying on the bridge of Arcola. He ordered that a heavy crate filled with this decorative biography be brought to him, and again the Balcombe children were invited to look and to admire. They were particularly impressed by the Egyptian Campaign, because the pyramids, the long-legged ibis birds and the smiling crocodiles lying in the mud of the river Nile, were so very fine. He gave a plate to Betsy Balcombe and one to her sister Jane, and over the following years a number of other people became owners of a piece of the Sèvres set, usually just because they had briefly expressed their admiration for it.

At the Pavilion Napoleon had already acquired the habit of staring at his possessions, mesmerised by the assoc-iations that were contained in each item, and looking at them as a person might look at a photograph of themselves as a child, or of friends who were long since dead. He would often give things away, impulsively and almost unthinkingly, as if he was suddenly aware that the thread that connected him with them was broken, and he could no longer claim these souvenirs as his own.

As well as bringing a quantity of objects with him from France, Napoleon had also brought a number of people, and just as the silver washstand and the golden snuff-boxes seemed out of place here in a ballroom belonging to an East India Company official, so also did the French count and the French general, the pastrycook, the groom, the two personal manservants and the others with their various wives and children who had come to join their master in his exile. All these men and women behaved as if they were still members of a large court, and even the most aristocratic amongst them treated Napoleon with a curious and relentless subservience. They spoke to him only when he addressed them, and they never challenged any of his requests or complained at a sudden act of impatience or anger. If, like that foolish emperor in the fairy story, he had been dressed in nothing but his own nakedness and had asked them to admire his fine clothes, they would have tried hard to chorus their approval. In China, in the early nineteenth century, a French missionary described how, 'When the emperor laughs, the mandarins in attendance laugh too; when he stops laughing, they stop. When he is sad their faces fall. One would think that their faces were on strings which the emperor could touch and set in motion at his pleasure' (Canetti, p. 417). Here, during the same period, but in another distant land, Napoleon's band of followers were obedient to similar rules. But the more fervently they tried to behave as if they were still in a palace or on a field of battle, the more stubbornly they had to ignore the sound of a chicken celebrating the laying of an egg, or the daily petty indignities that faced them on all sides.

Because the Pavilion was so small, Napoleon could only have a few of his people with him, and the remainder had to stay on at the house of Mr Porteous or at other boarding houses in Jamestown. During his first weeks as a guest of the Balcombes, he had with him two manservants, two cooks, a count and the count's young son. The count was called Emmanuel Auguste Dieudonné Marius Joseph de Las Cases. He was an intensely serious, small-boned, white-faced man in his early forties, even smaller than Napoleon himself, and stiff with the formality of his family background and the historic significance of being with the Emperor on St Helena. His ambition was to help Napoleon in writing a book about his imperial career, and already during the long sea journey to the island Napoleon had started a daily dictation, his voice sharp and impatient as he rushed through his memories, while Las Cases sat bent at a table, trying to keep pace with the spoken word. When Las Cases was summoned to the Pavilion he was eager to continue with the great work; they had only reached the Italian Campaign of 1796, and so many extraordinary years lay ahead of them both. He describes arriving at The Briars, and approaching the familiar figure of him 'who had filled ambassadors, princes, even kings with fear', and there he is, standing in the doorway of the Pavilion, with his hands clasped behind his back, staring at the mountains and whistling a tune from the French Vaudeville. He appears to be in a very good humour, almost skittish, and he shows his earnest scribe the two tiny rooms in the loft where Las Cases and his son were to take up their living quarters.

Precisely above the Emperor, a space seven foot square, where there was nothing but a bed without a single chair; that was where my lodging was, and my son's who was to have a mattress on the floor. Could we complain? We were so close to the Emperor that from where we were we could hear the sound of his voice, even his words! (Las Cases, vol. I, p. 159)

In between the dictations Las Cases wanted to talk about ideas and philosophy, the patterns that history makes as it moves through the centuries, but Napoleon really only wanted to talk about his own childhood. Perhaps it was the presence of the high mountains, or the quiet of the place, or the sound of farm animals, but something fixed his thoughts on the family home in Corsica, and made him resist all attempts to be dragged forward into adulthood.

Napoleon's two manservants, Marchand and St Denis, were also living at the Pavilion. Every morning they rubbed the body of the Emperor with eau-de-Cologne, and dressed him in his silks and satins, brushed his hair, polished his medals and his shoes with their golden buckles, and obeyed each new order. At night they slept like dogs, wrapped up in their cloaks and lying across the doorway, ready to stop any intruder who might try to enter, or to go and sit with their master if he was restless and could not sleep.

Then there was the cook Cipriani, who as it happened

had only a year to live, and the pastrycook Pierron; the two of them slept in a hut in the garden, and did their best to prepare imperial food in a little arbour near to the vegetable garden, and then to serve it with all the flourish and formality that was expected of them. Pierron managed to obtain the necessary ingredients for his work as the royal sweet-maker, and he used spun sugar to produce amber-coloured palaces and castles and triumphal arches, done in the neo-classical style of architecture which Napoleon had favoured when ordering new buildings to be erected in Paris and elsewhere. Cipriani prepared the main dishes, and when everything was ready he would bow low and announce, 'Your Majesty's dinner is served.' Then with his eyes averted to the ground he retreated backwards to the place on the lawn where a small table had been set out.

After a few weeks some soldiers came and erected a marquee next to the Pavilion, with a little covered way connecting the two constructions. Napoleon increased his household accordingly and sent for his lamplighter Rousseau to come and join him; this man proved very good at making toys to entertain the Balcombe children. Once he made a tiny carriage to which he harnessed six mice, but the mice were so afraid that they could not be persuaded to move until Napoleon suggested twisting the tails of the two leaders together, and then they ran. He also sent for another of his aristocratic companions to come and help with the work of transcribing the memoirs. This was General Baron de Gourgaud, who always felt that he was not being loved or appreciated enough by anybody, and clamoured for attention like a spoiled child. Napoleon had already moved his sleeping quarters to one end of the marquee, and Gourgaud was given a military campbed at the other end. The floor was the grass of the lawn, and one of the servants of the household cut the shape of a crown into the turf near the Emperor's bed, so that anyone who approached him had to step over this symbol of sovereignty, and at night it guarded him like a talisman to ward off evil spirits.

To see Napoleon in his white silk socks with his green silk jacket, and his troupe of obedient companions dancing in attendance around him, it is not difficult to understand why he said that he could not look forward into the unknown future without a sense of horror, and why if he looked back into the past his mind would not settle on his achievements as the ruler of an empire, but precipitated him into the middle of his own childhood. Of course he must whistle tunes from the Vaudeville, and play tricks on the people who try to please him, and mock others and himself as well. A fear must sit upon him, like those medieval paintings which show a devil with a spiny tail perched on the shoulder of a man or woman who is too preoccupied to notice the creature's presence.

During the first weeks of his captivity on the island, Napoleon is already hemmed in by boredom, just as he is hemmed in by the mountains, by the Atlantic Ocean and by the battalions of British soldiers who have been stationed on this small area of land to keep watch over him. He paces backwards and forwards through the days, trying to make time pass more quickly, and he cuts the days up into small sections, moving impatiently from dressing to eating, to walking, to playing chess, to dictating his memoirs, and then back to more talk, a change of clothes, more food, exercise, paperwork and talk, and finally a return to the sudden darkness and stillness of the night.

Only the children can help him step out of the pattern of monotony and evasion, and so, not surprisingly, he turns to them. The two Balcombe boys are in the same age-group as Napoleon's own son, the King of Rome, whose portrait hangs on the wall of the Pavilion. Once the boys have understood that this strange man who has come to live in the garden wants to play, they are happy to do so, and because they are still small they can clamber over him like puppies with a large dog. They examine his clothed body carefully: the rings on the fingers, the embroidered flurries on a jacket, the feel of the hair; they play with the medals that hang from his chest, and sometimes when they have admired a particularly fine embroidered decoration he asks their sister Betsy to bring him some scissors, so that he can cut a piece off and give it to them.

Betsy's sister Jane is older, and rather distant from the games, but Betsy herself clings on to the amphibious state between childhood and womanhood which allows her to be bad-mannered and rough, while keeping an edge of flirtatiousness. On the first evening at The Briars, when the family gathers around their foreign guest in the front parlour, Napoleon asks Betsy to sing a song at the piano and she gives a rendering of a sentimental Scottish ballad about love and nostalgia. He answers by humming his favourite song, 'Long Live Henry IV', and he hums it loudly and tunelessly and becomes so preoccupied with his own thoughts that he strides around the little room, ignoring the gaze of the strangers he has only met that afternoon.

'If the king had offered me Paris, his finest city,
But asked in return that I gave up my own true love,
I would say to the king, 'Take back your fine city!
I prefer my own true love,
I prefer my love.'

When he has finished with his pacing and his humming, he turns to Betsy and asks her if she liked his tune, and she says no, she did not.

During the days and weeks that followed Betsy became increasingly brazen in her treatment of this prisoner who had suddenly become part of her family life. Count de Las Cases and General Gourgaud, and all of the French servants watch incredulously at the way their master encourages this child to tease him and to flout his authority, but in their diaries and memoirs they avoid describing the games that are played in any detail, and refer to them only obliquely. 'The children,' says Gourgaud, 'call His Majesty Monsieur, and behave most shockingly . . . Betsy was today quite amazing towards the Emperor, but he did not seem to mind . . .' 'His Majesty says that he feels as if he is at a masked ball,' says Las Cases, but in all of his voluminous memoirs he never mentions the occasion when he punished Betsy for insolent behaviour by pushing her roughly against a steep bank, only to find in the next minute that Napoleon was holding him tightly by the shoulders while Betsy thumped his ears with her fists.

Betsy tells Napoleon that a certain Miss Legg is coming to the house and is very much afraid of that ogre of a military man called Bonaparte, so he goes to meet this girl with his hair ruffled up on end, his head lolling on one side and his face contorted, and when he is close to her he lets out a savage howl. The girl is terrified, and runs away, and he then turns on Betsy and howls at her too, but she is simply pleased by the game and the madness of the noise. Later there must have been many occasions at Longwood house, when ladies and gentlemen came to stare at him, or soldiers peered at him through keyholes and shuttered windows, when he wished that he could again let his head hang sideways, and his eyes roll, and could howl like a dog baying at the white disc of the moon.

Betsy was given permission to interrupt Napoleon at any time during the day, and so she would disturb the servants who guarded him as he dozed on a hot afternoon, and would burst into the privacy of the dictation sessions with Las Cases or Gourgaud in the grape arbour. They played at cards and he cheated; she taught him Blind Man's Buff and he cheated again, and she revenged herself by threatening him with his own sword, and by running off with a bundle of dictated memoirs.

It would seem that Napoleon was pleased with all the roughness and the taunting, except perhaps on one occasion. Betsy had told him quite a lot about how little English children who did not behave were warned that Boney would come to get them if they did not mend their ways. One day she showed him a mechanical child's toy, made of wood and produced in large numbers by a manufacturer in London. It showed him fat-bellied and wearing his three-cornered hat, standing on the bottom rung of a ladder. You pressed a button, and the little figure mounted jerkily up the steps, each of which was marked with the name of a country: Italy, Spain, Russia, Germany, and the topmost step was called St Helena. When he reached that his legs crumpled under him, and he toppled from the ladder and hung there like a spider suspended on its own thread.

CHAPTER VII

O that it were possible we might
But hold some two days conference
   with the dead!
From them I should learn somewhat, I
   am sure
I never shall know here.

          Webster, *Duchess of Malfi*

It's a very odd business trying to find out about Napoleon on the island of St Helena. You read a book by someone who seems to be honest and sensible and he says, 'Yes I was there and I spent a great deal of time with the Emperor, talking to him and listening to him – he gave me this golden buckle as a token of our friendship.' Then you read another book by another seemingly honest man and the author says, 'What him? He is an inveterate liar! Certainly he was on the island, but only for a few days, and if he saw Napoleon at all it was through the eyes of a telescope. The buckle? That was probably stolen, presuming of course that it is authentic, it looks to me as if it was made in England and might have belonged to an army officer.'

Mr William Warden, an English surgeon who was on the

ship that brought Napoleon to St Helena, wrote about the occasion when he arranged to visit the prisoner while he was still living at the Pavilion. Because he arrived early he went exploring, following the meandering goat tracks that criss-crossed the slopes of the mountains, and some distance from the house he unexpectedly came across Napoleon who was clattering over the rocks in his heavy riding boots. The Emperor was very friendly; he invited Mr Warden to join him at one of his favourite spots, and led him to a place where a wooden plank had been fixed as a bench between two boulders.

> On all sides rocks were piled on rocks to the height of a thousand feet above our heads, while there was an abyss of equal depth at our feet . . .
> 'Well,' said Napoleon with a smile, 'what say you to it? And can you think that your countrymen have treated me kindly?' (Warden, in Shorter, p. 215)

The two men met on several other occasions during those early months and they would talk at length about life, politics and history. Warden grew very fond of his unlikely companion and told a friend, 'He is only a man now, and will charm you; there is nothing about him to alarm.' When he got back to England he wrote a book about what had taken place and it was published anonymously under the title of *Letters from St Helena*. Some said that Napoleon thoroughly approved of the book and agreed with every word of it, but others were not so sure and one man who was on the island at that same time asserted that it was composed of nothing but cheap lies and propaganda since Warden had never had a single conversation with the Emperor and had picked up all his information second-hand. In this particular case I tend to trust the description of Napoleon clattering over the rocks and because of that I trust the rest of the narrative as well, but I might be wrong.

I went to see a man in his red wall-papered study with the letter N painted in gold above the bookcases and he told me that he probably knew more about Napoleon than anyone else in all the world. He certainly had amassed a large collection of books and papers and items relating to his subject. On his desk there was a marble bust of the Emperor done in the Roman style with a crown of laurel leaves around his wide white head. Nearby there was a plaster cast of the death mask and on the wall a piece of the cloak that had been worn at the Battle of Marengo, set in a pretty frame. He showed me several authentic signatures and documents and a little plastic doll wearing white britches and a black three-cornered hat. I asked him about a report I had read in a faded clipping from the *Morning Gazette* in which it was announced that Napoleon's favourite pet monkey had just arrived at Plymouth from St Helena and a famous artist was going to paint its portrait in oils. 'Rubbish,' he said. 'Napoleon never had a pet monkey on the island. He had no pets at all apart from the goldfish that died in the pond and the bedraggled birds in the aviary. And speaking of animals did you know that he was a hopeless horserider? He would sit hunched in the saddle, wobbling and sliding with every movement, and he often toppled to the ground. It's amazing that he was not once seriously hurt, just a few bruises.' I thought of the White Knight in *Through the Looking Glass* who fell backwards from his horse when it started to move and forwards over its head when it stopped; he also miraculously escaped injury.

We went on to discuss a number of people who had been on St Helena when Napoleon was there and had all left some sort of written account of what they had seen and heard. I learnt that Dr O'Meara was honest no matter what everyone said to the contrary; Dr Antommarchi was stupid and greedy but he was not bad; Governor Lowe became increasingly paranoid; General Gourgaud was probably a latent homosexual and Count de Las Cases was even shorter than Napoleon which meant that he could not have been much more than five feet high. I asked him if he himself had ever thought of visiting St Helena, since the island and its prisoner had occupied his mind for so long, and he said no, he knew the place so well that going there could only be a disappointment. One last question and that was about the diary that was kept by Betsy Balcombe during Napoleon's first three years of exile. He assured me that such a diary did not exist, and even if it did but had somehow escaped his knowledge, there was no point in my consulting it since there was nothing that a fourteen-year-old girl could possibly contribute to our understanding of the final stage in the life of the Emperor. He felt that the book she had written many years later, as Mrs Abell, *Recollections of the Emperor Napoleon during the first three years of his captivity*, was an extremely suspect work, and much of it was the product of the fantasy of a sad middle-aged woman who was short of cash and wanted the status of being in the public eye. He did however have a first edition of this book if I would care to see it. It was a very fine copy in perfect condition, signed by the author, with hand-coloured engravings and stiff thick leather bindings.

Before I go any further let me try to explain something. Napoleon has preoccupied a great many people for a long time. More books have been written about him than about any other human being, alive or dead, real or imaginary, and this has surrounded him with a babbling cacophony of voices, all competing with each other for attention and all busily contradicting one another. It is not difficult to see him stretched out vast and still and indeed very much like an island, while a restless crowd moves this way and that across his body: measuring him, examining him, burrowing under his skin and breaking into his bones in an effort to discover something more about him. It is not only the books that have proliferated; there are also vast collections of items which all claim to be intimately related to him. I have already seen four beds in which he is supposed to have died, and numerous locks of hair taken from his head, bone from his rib, wood from his coffin, cups from which he drank and chairs on which he sat and thought.

I come upon Napoleon as an outsider. Before starting on this book I had presumed rather vaguely that St Helena was somewhere in the Mediterranean and the people there spoke French – or was it Italian? I had heard that Napoleon was poisoned by the arsenic in the wallpaper that lined his bedroom and I had wondered, but never found out, if this was supposed to have been a case of murder or an unfortunate accident. There was a radio documentary I once listened to, based I think on the journals of Dr Antommarchi, that had left me with the impression that whatever Napoleon had been like before he came to St Helena, once he was there on the island he was utterly and irredeemably mad. I carried, as I suppose many people must carry, a couple of images of this most famous historic figure. In the first I could see him in black and white like a cartoon character, stiff-legged and seeming to lean forward into a strong wind, with one hand pushed into his tightly-fitting waistcoat as if he was trying to feel for his own heartbeat. The second is based on a painting which shows him young and handsome, riding into battle on a wild white horse with a blue cloak and a red flag flying, and man and horse both have a look of death and victory in their eyes.

But if I pause to wonder why I ever came to be working through the books and the papers, the diaries and journals that are all in some way to do with this one man, then perhaps I must go back many years to an occasion when I visited a little town somewhere in the south of France, I forget its name, and I was told that the local museum possessed the pickled testicles of Napoleon Bonaparte, floating into eternity in a sealed glass jar filled with pure alcohol. There was something so utterly incongruous about the idea of such a bizarre and savage relic being given a home in the respectful atmosphere of a civic museum. I imagined afternoon visitors pausing to read the caption under the display before moving on to admire paintings, hats and chairs. Have the testicles of anyone else, a saint, perhaps, or a tyrant, been preserved in this way, I wonder? And what would Napoleon think, if walking along the endless corridors of museum collections dedicated to him and his achievements, he had encountered these strange and disembodied items that had also once belonged to him. Now that I know more, but by no means everything, about what happened to him on St Helena, I can on the one hand doubt the authenticity of this particular relic, but I can also easily accept that it might well be exactly what it claims to be.

After this wide circle of thought let me return to Betsy Balcombe's account of the Napoleon she once knew. The diary does exist and it has apparently made its way into a collection of papers and documents that lie in the archive department of an art gallery in Melbourne, Australia. It is not a narrative by any means, just a few brief jottings that leap over the months and ignore a great deal of what is happening in the outside world. Betsy complains about the noise made by the cannon when Napoleon's ship moves into the harbour at Jamestown, and then she is busy with thoughts about a dress she hopes to have made for her. She is pleased with the Emperor when he plays wild games with her and her sister and brothers and is generous with sugarplums, and she resents him when he avoids her and spends his time dictating his memoirs to Las Cases. But using this diary and Betsy's own book, as well as a few other scattered references, it is possible to reconstruct some of the things that happened during the first seven weeks of Napoleon's imprisonment.

These events emerge as a collection of curious stories, little anecdotes bundled together in a pack, but then as Napoleon said, being at the Pavilion was like being at a masked ball and at this stage he was still presuming that at some point the music would stop and everyone could return to their accustomed lives. For the moment the game was the thing.

During those early weeks the complex machinery that was going to hold the prisoner in place was only just beginning to be set in motion. There were no armed sentries patrolling the area that contained him and the sudden influx of new soldiers were all busy establishing themselves at Deadwood camp or elsewhere on the other side of the mountains. As the wife of a young army captain explained in a letter sent to her aunt in England:

> Wooden Barracks are to be erected in the Camp for our Regiment as soon as practicable; but to drag the materials up these perpendicular Mountains on Men's shoulders will require time. There will be no room for the Married Officers who are therefore preparing to build Huts against the periodic Rains which will render living in a Tent unwholesome as well as uncomfortable.
>
> There are such horrible quantities of Fleas that my Life has been nigh tormented away. If I take a walk on the Grass I come home literally covered from head to foot, and am obliged to pull off my clothes and throw them outside the Tent. (Mrs Younghusband, p. 152)

For the time being visitors could call on Napoleon without obtaining an official pass, and a steady stream of the more wealthy islanders, army officers and their wives (including the flea-ridden Mrs Younghusband), and travellers whose ship had been allowed to stop at Jamestown, made their way to The Briars, like sightseers eager to feast their eyes on a famous monument. Not surprisingly Napoleon became quite daunted by the sight of these little parties of total strangers who came to see him with nothing to say except a few lame questions. After one polite and particularly meaningless encounter he was assured that 'the ladies were particularly gratified . . . to find him so different a person from what he had been represented. To which he replied, "I suppose they imagined that I was some strange animal, with two great horns sticking out of my head." ' *Morning Chronicle* 24 July 1816)

Sometimes he refused to be seen and once he tried to escape an impending encounter by jumping over a fence, but he had the misfortune of falling backwards into a prickly-pear bush and needed to be rescued. One eager gentleman who failed to obtain an interview wrote in a letter to *The Times*:

> We were of course very anxious to get a peep at the great Napoleon . . . I slipt behind a bush a little way from the walk where he was to pass. He passed several times within a few feet of us; we had a most distinct view of him. There was nothing however in his appearance, at all indicative of the great qualities he possesses. (*The Times*, 17 January 1816)

He was free to go walking in whichever direction he chose; no sentries stopped and questioned him along the way and during those first weeks while the weather was still tolerable, he was often to be seen going up the narrow goat paths that led into the mountains. He also went riding regularly on his horse called Hope, although for these expeditions he was always accompanied by an army officer called Captain Poppleton. Betsy tells the story of how he once escaped from his guard by veering off the track and urging his horse up the mountainside, sending down a cascade of loose rocks. Poppleton did not give chase, but returned alone and reported to the admiral that he had lost the Emperor. By then Napoleon was already back at the Pavilion, eating his dinner and proud of his joke.

For as long as Napoleon felt that he was a guest at a masked ball he maintained a disconcertingly light-hearted mood that sometimes bordered on hysteria. He could be seen puffing across the garden, his movements, according to Betsy, 'something between a strut and a waddle', with four children close at his heels shouting and screaming in their excitement. They clambered over him and called him Boney which made him laugh, and together with them he would set off to tease some of his own dignified companions and to plan tricks that would make fools of them. When Betsy wanted to punish him for something he had said that upset her, she got hold of his sword – made of gold and decorated with imperial bees – and she chased him and Gourgaud into a corner of the sitting-room, threatening to kill them both, her screams only drowned by his laughter. When her arm finally tired she returned the sword to its owner and he pinched her nose and kissed her on both cheeks telling her that she was brave but not wise.

Betsy complimented him on his horseriding and at once he ordered Hope to be brought to him in the garden and he mounted and displayed his skill by wheeling and turning in short fast circles on the lawn like a bird might dance before its mate. Seeing him manage to calm a young and nervous horse, she tells him that she thinks he would have made a very good horsebreaker, to which he replies, 'Men and horses have a similar mentality.'

There was an elderly man called Old Huff who was employed as a tutor for the two Balcombe boys. He was convinced that it was his duty to free the Emperor and he became so obsessed with the idea and with each new plan he thought up that everyone connected with Napoleon would avoid him whenever he approached. Then one morning he committed suicide and it was ordered that his body should be buried at a place near The Briars where three roads intersected. Ghosts are very active and dangerous in St Helena and the servants, the children and the slaves all refused to go near the spot where Old Huff was lying. Napoleon got caught up in the talk about suicides and ghosts. He told Betsy how he would have killed himself if he had decided to, he told her about the spirits of dead men that haunt battlefields crying for their lost limbs, and the ghosts that were to be found on the island of Corsica. Several times, just as night was falling, he would call out from the verandah of the Pavilion, 'Betsee, Old Huff, Old Huff!' and Mrs Balcombe would comfort her daughter saying, 'Don't worry my dear, it's only the Emperor.' He even arranged for a slave to wrap himself in a white sheet and come sliding through the darkness towards the house, moaning and sighing, until the spell was broken by harsh laughter from among the bushes.

Napoleon stayed in this strange hilarity until 19 November. The days were becoming increasingly hot and humid and the nights were very cold. He had taken to getting up at four in the morning in order to work in the arbour in the garden before the sun appeared over the mountains, and then like an old man he would sit there, dozing and waking and dozing again. Betsy had permission to disturb him at all times and she would come and stand next to him and hold his hand until he woke. Maybe it was the weather, or the length of time that had already passed so slowly and the immeasurable time that still lay ahead, but he developed a feverish cold and with that he became withdrawn and sad. His servants hovered around his bed watching him and worrying over him. Mrs Balcombe offered him a drink made out of honey and a doctor suggested more violent remedies, but he refused to take anything except the liquorice which he said was the only medicine he had ever trusted. By 28 November he had recovered his strength, but his mood had changed.

During the first week of December it was announced that Longwood was almost ready for its new tenant, although the rooms still smelt strongly of paint. On the evening of 8 December Napoleon was over at the Balcombes' house. Supper was finished and the children were eager to persuade him to play a game of Blind Man's Buff. When they explained the game to him he realised that it was a version of *collon maillard*, and he did not want to take part, saying that the last time he had played it was at Malmaison, that palace in France where he had once lived. But the children were insistent and finally he agreed and carefully prepared the little strips of paper, writing *La Mort* on one of them. Betsy was chosen to be blindfolded, and in her diary she describes the game as being 'fast and furious'. Napoleon sheltered behind the ladies, crouched down to be the same height as the little boys and scampered across the room laughing uncontrollably. Then abruptly the game was brought to an end by the unexpected arrival of the English admiral and Napoleon's general, Bertrand. The admiral wished to discuss the plans for moving to Longwood at the earliest opportunity. Napoleon said he would receive his visitor in the Pavilion and he excused himself and left the house. He was unwilling to make the move at such short notice and especially since the smell of fresh paint at Longwood would make him sick. However the admiral was determined in his purpose; if Napoleon and his companions were not packed and ready within a couple of days then he would send a hundred soldiers to The Briars, to set up camp in a small circle around the Pavilion.

CHAPTER VIII

I have always feared the sound of the
wind beyond anything. In my hell it
would always blow a gale.

R. L. Stevenson, *Notebooks*

There was a London hospital near where I lived as a child
which was called The Royal Hospital for Incurables. Its cul-
de-sac of a name was written in big letters on a board
outside the gate through which new patients entered. You
must change character going through a gate like that, try to
wrap yourself up in a cloak of madness or senility or some
other disguise that should help to carry you forward into a
future that has no visible landmarks, and no point of
change or movement except the knowledge that death will
come eventually and bring an end to life. There are those
who choose slowness as a way of hiding, and they become
suspended in their movements like reptiles waiting for the
sun to warm their blood before they have the energy to
turn the head or raise a foot off the ground. I once stood
inside a glass cage filled with iguanas from the Galapagos

Islands, and one of them kept falling asleep with the effort of eating a lettuce leaf; it made me think of my grandfather, the nurse slapping his cheeks in the hope that he might open his eyes for a moment and say hello or goodbye. Then there are the fast, impatient ones, pacing this way and that, emptying waste paper baskets, picking like hens at the corner of a sleeve, tormented by the knowledge that it's getting very late and there is still so much to do. I used occasionally to visit the poet Robert Graves during his final years, his long imperial face pale and sad and he standing in his own sitting-room touching the stones of the fireplace and saying, 'Come along now, I want to go home. Oh let's go home, do hurry, it's time to go.' Or that meeting with an old lady with a schoolgirl's face and she sitting on her bed in a little room in a private nursing home, her hands clasped around her knees and her body rocking from side to side as she sang,

> 'Forty-four and forty-five
> Am I dead or am I alive?
> I know but I don't care
> I know about despair.'

Napoleon was just forty-six when he came to St Helena; he had celebrated his birthday on the ship that brought him here. While he was still staying at the Pavilion he was new to his own captivity and had not yet learnt to recognise himself as a prisoner, but as soon as he moved to Longwood, the house and its surroundings and the pattern of existence that it offered, forced him to see things very differently and quickly affected his appearance and the way that he behaved from day to day.

He was ready to change houses on the morning of Sunday 10 December. The weather was fine and he got up early and went out into the garden so that his servants could again pack up his furniture and other possessions and set them out on the lawn. There were very few mules or other pack animals on the island and for some reason a number of Chinese men who had recently arrived from the province of Canton were used to 'perform the office of horses'. I imagine Napoleon watching as these small, dignified and strong-boned men, dressed in their loose robes, loaded his campbed with its green curtains, his silver washstand, his boxes of plates and ornaments, on to little wooden carts and then dragged them up the mountainside and out of sight. Later he would employ several Chinese at Longwood and he grew very fond of them in spite of the confusion and distance of language. They made him intricate wooden puzzles to play with, a painted screen to hide his bed from the guards who sometimes peered in through the window, and a little chess set carved out of black ebony and white willow with all the black pawns made to look like portraits of the Emperor wearing his three-cornered hat.

He breakfasted at a table set out in the walled vegetable garden, with Las Cases and Mr Balcombe to keep him company, and according to Las Cases he was 'in charming spirits, and his conversation was very lively'. He went for a walk along the now familiar goat paths and when he was back in the garden an English sailor appeared at the gate and stared at him silently and solemnly, holding a bunch of wild flowers in his hand which he seemed to want to offer as a gift, but losing courage he bowed and disappeared as suddenly as he had come. Napoleon changed into a coat of green satin, and with the sash of the Legion of Honour tied across his chest and his hat on his head, he waited for the moment of departure. At two o'clock the English admiral arrived, along with a number of English officers in their bright red uniforms and the members of Napoleon's suite who had been staying in Jamestown.

Napoleon said goodbye to Betsy, gave her a sweet box and told her that she must persuade her father to bring her regularly to Longwood. Mrs Balcombe was ill in bed and he rushed up to her room, sat with her for a while and presented her with a gold snuff-box decorated with his initials, telling her that he wished he did not have to leave for he had been happy here.

A new horse had been brought for him from the Cape, and although neither its name nor its colour is mentioned, it was described as being small and sprightly. There is a horse like this one must have been, a little white Arab called The Vizier, which stands stiff-legged and wide eyed in a glass case in the Army Museum in Paris. It has the Imperial crown branded on to its rump and it is so delicate and gentle-faced that it looks as if it has been crossed with a deer or a racing dog while its smallness makes one realise how small Napoleon must have been. He mounted and set off for a second time up the track that led to Deadwood Plain, and many people had gathered along the way to watch him passing. The admiral rode at one side of him and General Bertrand at the other, while a group of English officers escorted the party. The track led to a gate in the unfinished wall surrounding Longwood. A guard of soldiers was waiting for them there and as the party approached the gate they beat out a salute on their drums that must have sounded as much like a warning as a welcome. The little horse shied at the sudden noise and had to be coaxed and spurred forward through the gate, and it is said that everyone present took this as a sign and glanced uneasily at each other.

Longwood had changed considerably since the last time Napoleon had seen it. Every day for the past seven weeks two to three hundred sailors had been at work carrying loads of timber and building materials, wallpaper and wallhangings, curtains and shutters, furniture, roofing tar, cement and paint, everything that could be used to enlarge the cramped structure of the house and to hide the strange nakedness of its interior. A ship's carpenter, Mr Cooper, and his assistant, Lieutenant Blood, as well as a number of other helpers were still busy with the task of trying to turn a summer residence that had been used by a man and a woman and a few servants, into a permanent home for an Emperor and a further fifty-one other individuals who were going to be cooped up under the same roof throughout the year. And since this strangely inhospitable house was to become so saturated with the presence of Napoleon and the assortment of people who lived with him there, and since he developed such an intimate knowledge of all of its contained spaces – the view from one window, the damp in one wall, a chimney that always smoked, the hollow chambers beneath the floors where the rats danced like carefree rabbits – it is perhaps a good idea to begin by examining the house carefully, moving from room to room.

The previous occupier, Mr Skelton, had attached a drawing-room at right-angles to the front of the house, and had also established a simple kitchen, servants' quarters and privies at the back, on the other side of a small enclosed courtyard which had previously been used for cattle. Under the direction of the admiral, who drew up the plans himself and even helped with some of the manual work, another room and a glassed-in verandah had been added to Mr Skelton's drawing-room, making the building into a curious T-shaped design, and a series of little wooden compartments were still in the process of being constructed behind the kitchen. When Napoleon arrived they were busy putting on the roofing of tarred felt, but it would be almost a year before all the plans were completed and Mr Blood and Mr Cooper could go home.

You walked up a flight of five steps on to the verandah and then through a door that led into the entrance room. It was a spacious area, twenty-six feet long and nineteen feet wide, but it had the disadvantage of being made of pinewood, and when the sun beat upon it, it became unbearably hot. The walls had been painted a pale green. There were two sash windows that looked out at that profile of a man's head called the Barn, and three windows that faced the island's highest mountain, Diana's Ridge, where the outline of High Knoll Fortress could be seen; a telescope was needed to watch the soldiers stationed there, and to see the array of cannons. All the windows in this room were fitted with wooden shutters and later Napoleon arranged for holes to be cut in them so that he could gaze out at the world which surrounded him without being seen. The holes are still there to be viewed by curious visitors, but the original shutters, along with the window frames and most of the walls, were eaten by termites in the 1860s. When Napoleon first saw this room it contained a piano, a couple of sofas and some small tables and chairs, but in a little while a large mahogany billiard table was due to arrive from England and it then dominated the space, although Napoleon himself did not enjoy the game and he used the sticks as walking canes and measuring rods and would try to bounce the balls into the pockets by hand. There would also soon be a globe of the heavens and a globe of the world, standing like guards one on either side of the door.

The next room was the drawing-room, decorated with pale yellow Chinese wallpaper and lit by two west-facing windows that also looked out at the fortress. A replica of this room can be seen in the Army Museum, near where the horse stands poised and still in his glass box, because during the last days of his life Napoleon had his bed moved here and this is where he died. You pass the horse and a few other display cabinets and you come to a heavy green curtain which draws back to reveal an interior, glass-fronted like an aquarium. Two campbeds are there, a couple of painted chairs and a threadbare carpet. The pillows on both beds are surprisingly high and a few clothes – britches, a shirt and a jacket – have been laid out carefully in readiness for the next morning. The two windows with their white muslin curtains look out on to an enlarged black-and-white photograph of the surrounding landscape. But for the moment the room was furnished with armchairs, folding tables and card tables, ready for a group of people to sit and play games, to read and to talk.

The dining-room was part of the old building. It was extremely dark since it had lost its main windows when the extension was built and now its only source of light came from a glass panel in a door leading to the garden. The original plan was to have the new room as a dining-room and this one could then have been the topographic room, with Napoleon busy with his maps and battle campaigns in a dim obscurity that was never shifted by the daylight. However it quickly became apparent that this was not possible, and a large table, a sideboard and ten chairs were moved in. Several people have described the experience of taking an evening meal here, with so many candles burning in the darkness that their little flames made the air 'as hot as an oven'. During mealtimes the rats could be heard going about their business; their holes had perforated the floor like a sieve, and the servants nailed pieces of tin over each new hole.

One door from the dining-room led into what would become the library, and one on the other side to an area that Napoleon referred to as 'my Interior' – a little study, a bedroom, a bathroom and a room for whichever of his two manservants was in attendance. The bedroom had a narrow window facing north-east and looking out on to the lawn. The walls were hung with a pale yellow cloth from Nanking in China, and bordered with a red flowered paper. There was a wooden fireplace painted grey, a chest of drawers, an old sofa covered with white cotton, an easy chair and a straight-backed chair. Napoleon's servant Marchand had gone ahead of the party to prepare his master's bedroom in readiness for his arrival. Two silver candlesticks, a silver cup and an incense burner had been set on the mantelpiece. On the walls were hung the portraits of Napoleon's young son, the King of Rome, shown sitting on a sheep, his mother, his first wife, and his second wife with her child in her arms. A silver alarm clock that had once belonged to Frederick the Great and which Napoleon had taken as a souvenir from the battlefield of Potsdam, hung on one side of the mantelpiece, and on the other side, for the sake of symmetry, a little golden watch with a chain made from the hair of his second wife, Marie-Thérèse. Here again was the silver washstand and travelling case and one of the two campbeds, set against the wall. A second bed was in the study and when Napoleon could not sleep he would move from one to the other during the night. The study also contained a writing table, chairs, and a makeshift bookcase. An external gallery behind the bedroom had been turned into a bathing chamber where the ship's carpenter had built and installed a long wooden trough lined with lead and looking very like a coffin. At first water was heated in the garden outside and passed through the window in buckets, although later a complicated boiler was installed.

Across the inner courtyard where the rats were said to move about in droves even in the daylight there was a little kitchen with a cracked stove where the cook, the pastry cook and the sweet maker continued with their work of producing sauces and mousses, an island of meringue floating on a sea of egg custard, a castle of spun sugar. Las Cases and his son had been allocated a room behind the kitchen, but when the stoves were lit the walls became too hot, and Napoleon moved them into an extension of the library. Some of the servants slept in the garret under the roof of the old building, with the ceilings too low to stand upright and the heat on the tarred paper in the roof making a sweltering atmosphere. Others, including the Irish doctor O'Meara who had become Napoleon's personal

doctor, General Gourgaud and the army officer, Poppleton, who had to keep watch on the Emperor, slept in tents
in the garden while the carpenters continued with their
work, and the carpenters themselves slept in a tent made
out of an old sail. Montholon, his wife and young child
were temporarily in the library, while Bertrand and his
wife had managed to take on a little house at Hutt's Gate.

The admiral led Napoleon around the house, pointing
out every detail of the work that had been done and
explaining what was to be done in the near future.
Napoleon seemed quite satisfied, and the admiral, when
he returned to Jamestown that evening, expressed himself
very relieved that everything had gone so well. At six
o'clock Napoleon retired to his room with Las Cases. He
asked if he looked as tired as he felt and said he would like
a bath. Las Cases stayed talking with him while he lay in
the water. On the following day, early in the morning, he
made an inspection of the outside of Longwood, the land
around it, the view in each direction.

A low white fence surrounded the area that was called
the garden, but as yet nothing was growing there except
rough grass. Diana's Ridge with its fortress lay to the west,
while in front of the house and about one mile away, the
Fifty-Third Regiment was already stationed. A second
regiment was established at Hutt's Gate, and about six
hundred paces from the house at the point where the gate
opened into the wall, a new guardhouse had been built for
the soldiers who kept watch there. Napoleon had been told
that he could walk within the area contained by the four-
mile-long wall without being escorted by an officer, but
because there were so few trees and the land was mostly
flat, there was nowhere he could go without being in full
sight of the soldiers. Already there were pickets of soldiers
posted on every vantage point, on every road, even on the
little goat paths. Over the following years a number of
those standing guard in awkward places lost their lives

when they were blown over precipices by strong winds. While Napoleon was making his first exploration of this area a sentry stopped him and demanded to know his intentions. He passed by the rough barracks where the Chinese labourers were housed and stopped there to try to talk to some of them. He looked at a farm where a few sheep were raised, and a vegetable garden belonging to the East India Company which was called Mulberry Gut and was situated in a hollow between two ravines which kept it sheltered from the winds blowing at all times during the day and the night.

That evening at nine o'clock fifty-two sentries obeyed their instructions and entered Longwood's garden. Some of them positioned themselves around the house while the others toured the inner perimeter of the fence, shouting greetings and brief exchanges to each other in the darkness as they waited for the approach of dawn.

CHAPTER IX

'And ever since that,' the Hatter went
on in a mournful tone, 'he won't do a
thing I ask. It's always six o'clock
now.'

Lewis Carroll,
Alice's Adventures in Wonderland

The Mad Hatter's watch stopped working and neither best
butter nor hot tea could mend it; so time stood still and he
and his two companions crowded themselves at one end of
a long table and drank tea and quarrelled all through the
blank succession of the days. When Alice arrived as an
unexpected guest they bombarded her with riddles that
had no answers and stories that had no endings and the
Mad Hatter became increasingly irritable and aggressive
while the March Hare lapsed into vague despair and the
Dormouse drifted in and out of sleep. When she got up to
leave they were too busy with each other to notice that she
was going.

For Napoleon and the mixed collection of people who
lived with him at Longwood, time was equally stubborn
and unmoving and the awful spectre of life as an endless

tea party was never very far away. In the island world that surrounded them there were no seasons to distinguish the gradual evolution of the year and no climatic patterns that could be predicted or relied upon since rain, wind, sun and mist followed a seemingly haphazard sequence and trees and plants were always simultaneously in bud, flower and fruit. With the first glimmering of the dawn a cannon was fired from High Knoll or Alarm Hill and its roar could be heard again at noon and at sunset, while the intermediary stages of each day were marked out by sentries marching stiff-legged to vantage points in the landscape – changing duty, presenting arms, firing rifles, sitting, standing, waiting, watching Longwood House. The old telegraphic relay system that had been installed by a previous governor was now fully operational and at some time during the morning a line of coloured flags was hoisted up on a high wire to communicate certain basic information from Deadwood Plain to the governor's residence on the other side of the mountains. Yellow, black, red, green, white: General Bonaparte is well; General Bonaparte is out but within the boundary wall; General Bonaparte is unwell and has not been seen. Blue was the colour of escape. This blue flag would have brought the entire military machinery to its feet with cannons roaring and guns primed for action, but over all the years it was never once used.

Every hour of every day Napoleon had nothing to do but eat and sleep and find some form of amusement that could serve to hold his mind steady. Everything that he chose to do, whether it was to sit in his bath for longer than usual, lose at cards, change the colour of his jacket or laugh loudly at supper, was watched and reported on, and since he knew that he could not avoid this scrutiny he answered it like an actor on a well-lit stage playing before a crowded auditorium. Ritual and the strictest rules of correct behaviour were to be maintained at all times when he was in the public eye, and in spite of the rats under the floor and the wind and rain working their way through the thinly protected roof, this place called Longwood House must be made to seem like an imperial palace occupied and controlled by an emperor. No one who entered these rooms was expected to speak unless spoken to, sit unless given a command, or do anything else that might suggest that they were independent of Napoleon's pervading presence. Even the four aristocratic officers and their two aristocratic wives who had chosen to accompany their Emperor in his exile, spoke to His Majesty only in a muted whisper, removed their hats in his presence even if it was cold and wet and were quick to obey his erratic commands without question or complaint. They tended to compete with one another in trying to please Napoleon, and this created an edge of rivalry and resentment that often erupted into bitter quarrels. And because there was nothing to do and nowhere to go, boredom could easily turn into hysteria. 'It would be nice,' remarked Napoleon during the first month of his captivity at Longwood, 'to fall asleep and not wake up for a year or two. Then we would find some big changes in our lives.' (Gourgaud, p. 32)

Every evening before dinner the ladies appeared in the drawing-room in their finest gowns, their necks and shoulders bare, their jewellery glistening and their hair twisted and curled into shape, and the gentlemen joined them in formal splendour, dressed in military uniforms, their heads held erect by stiff high collars. This little group and any extra invited guests were expected to help pass the time from sunset until Napoleon was ready to go to bed, and although he might decide abruptly to disappear at nine o'clock he often sought entertainment until late into the night. 'Come,' he would say, 'ladies, gentlemen, let us go to the theatre,' and standing in front of the makeshift bookcase he would select a volume of some classical play, and begin to read from it in a steady and monotonous voice.

> He had no ear for rhythm and would often add one or two syllables to a line, not realising what he was doing. During such readings the ladies would stifle their yawns, but let him notice one and out of spite he would hand the volume to the culprit begging her to continue. He himself would then promptly fall asleep. (Madame Montholon, in Aubry, p. 162)

The men were supposed to remain standing throughout the evening unless they were playing at a board game. 'At times they would almost faint from weariness,' Madame Montholon remembered. 'General Gourgaud used to lean against the door. I saw him turn pale on some occasions as he watched a game of chess' (quoted in Aubry, p. 160). The servants would be in attendance as well, dressed in full livery with silver and gold lace, green satin waistcoat for one, black satin britches for another, and they too must stand and sway and wait in silence until something was demanded of them. The rules that governed this tiny kingdom were established within the first month, and they remained basically unchanged until Napoleon had died and the house was again empty.

It was the prerogative of the Emperor to talk to everyone he met as if he was thinking aloud, and rather than follow through a conversation step by step he would ask questions on whatever subjects floated up in his mind, whether it was the number of cows kept on the island, the length of time it took an English officer to eat his dinner, or 'Are you fond of flowers? Do you know Lord Kinnaird? How many Scotch peers are not peers in Parliament?' (Lady Malcolm, p. 47). Dr Warden, who claimed to have had many long conversations with Napoleon, described a supper at Longwood during which his host asked a succession of questions about dysentery and other related diseases while eating the food set before him at a tremendous speed:

> Have you examined them after death?
> What is the appearance?
> What is death – or how do you define death?
> When does the soul quit the body?
> When do you suppose the soul enters the body?
> (Warden, in Shorter, p. 220)

Mrs Younghusband described what must have been a typical social evening at Longwood in January 1816, a little more than a month after Napoleon had moved into his new residence. When she arrived at seven o'clock, Napoleon was walking in the garden, but he came quickly to the house to greet her and the other invited guest, Sir George Bingham. A grand piano had been delivered the day before and he was eager to know if she thought it was as good or perhaps better than the one at Plantation House. He asked her to play him a tune and sing him some Italian songs, but before she began he would read the words aloud to her since that might improve her pronunciation. She had just completed two short pieces when he asked her to join him at a card game called Tric Trac, and when she failed to understand the rules he wanted her to teach him the English version of Backgammon, but his concentration did not last and he gave up after a few minutes. At that moment Cipriani, the maître d'hôtel, threw open the doors that led to the dining-room and announced that dinner was served. Napoleon led the way and sat at the head of the table with his back to the fireplace and his two man-servants Marchand and St Denis, dressed in green, white, black and gold, standing on either side of his chair like ceremonial lions. Mrs Younghusband was shown to a seat on the Emperor's right, and Sir George Bingham, General and Madame Bertrand, Count and Countess Montholon, General Gourgaud and Count de Las Cases followed in single file and in what was considered the order of their rank and social status. That blind room with no windows to the outside world was illuminated by dozens of candles and the flickering light ignored the threadbare carpets and the pale cotton cloth on the walls and concentrated instead on the eagles' heads which decorated the gold and silver plate, the silver and gold of the cutlery, the bright colours of the porcelain, the shimmer of glass. Five courses were served in such quick succession that the whole meal was over in less than half an hour, and a variety of stewed fruits was presented in magnificent Sèvres bowls 'representing the great battlefields of Egypt and Europe'.

During the whole of the Dinner no-one uttered a syllable above their breath excepting the Emperor and myself, and for the greater part of the time a dead silence prevailed among the party. Bonaparte asked me a number of questions respecting the East Indies and several about our Camp. (Mrs Younghusband, p. 150)

After the meal Napoleon wanted to play *reversie*. It was a card game that he used to play as a child, and now that he had rediscovered it he felt sure that it could keep him amused for hours on end, just as it had once done long ago. The winner was the one who managed to lose the most cards and as always Napoleon cheated; for politeness' sake those playing with him pretended not to notice. During the first months at Longwood he played the game repeatedly, until he had tired it of all its possibilities.

He made it so complex that I have seen fifteen to eighteen thousand counters in use at once. The Emperor's aim was always to make the *reversie*, that is to make every trick, which is no easy matter. (Las Cases, vol. I, p. 275)

On this particular evening he grew very excited and while the cards were being dealt he sang some of his favourite songs:

'My friends let us live like good Christians
Believe me it is the path we all must take
For each man, in the end, must submit to his duty.'

The party was brought to a close at eleven o'clock and Mrs Younghusband went back to her flea-ridden camp while Napoleon returned to his private rooms and whatever restless night lay ahead of him.

He tended to wake at five or six in the morning, sometimes brought to his senses by the sound of the cannon, sometimes anticipating its dull explosion by half an hour or more. Either Marchand or St Denis would be sleeping on a carpet at the foot of the bed and they were ready for the first signs that would tell them to let in the day. The shutters and the white curtains were opened, and the green drapes that hung around the bed were pulled back to reveal the sunlight, the mist or the dark rain of the morning. Napoleon dressed himself in white trousers and white silk socks and drank a cup of black coffee and then his two servants were ready to help him with the morning's toilet. The silver washstand was set before the open window, and one servant held the soap and the razor while the other held up the mirror. He shaved the side of his face closest to the window and then turned the other way and the mirror was again set before him. The pale and almost hairless skin of his torso was rubbed with eau-de-Cologne or, when supplies of that had run out, with lavender water, and his servants were taught to scrub him with a soft brush. 'Rub harder,' he would tell them. 'Rub as if you were scrubbing a donkey.' Then, cleanly shaved and sweet smelling, he put on a white shirt and red braces and a long white dressing gown that looks like a doctor's coat as it now hangs stiffly in a glass case in a museum. If the weather was fine he might go for a ride and on returning he would begin a new instalment of his dictation of his past life. Since arriving at Longwood all four officers had become involved in writing down these dictations and the one who was summoned would announce to his companions, 'I am off to the wars. His Majesty is at this very moment reorganising his army.' Each officer had been given a different stage of history, so that Las Cases was still busy revising the Italian Campaign of 1796, Bertrand was in Egypt in 1798, Gourgaud was deep in the complexities and failures of the Battle of Waterloo, while Montholon was obliged to move backwards and forwards across this dense sweep of time. Marchand was writing down Napoleon's interpretation of Cæsar's military campaigns and St Denis had the task of copying out all these accounts, so that they were united by his clear and easily legible script.

This first immersion in thoughts about the past was interrupted by breakfast, served either on a little table in Napoleon's 'Interior', or taken with the rest of the household in the drawing-room. Then there was often a further dictation in what became known as the billiard room at the front of the house, which had the advantage of remaining cool in the mornings although it still smelled strongly of paint, especially if the weather was damp. Napoleon would sometimes interrupt the flow of his narrative and set his eyeglass at one of the holes cut in the closed slats of the venetian blinds, and from there he could stare out at the sea in the distance. During those early months there was still the possibility of being rescued, and each new ship carried hope in its black silhouette as it approached the island and disappointment as it turned to sail away again. Napoleon paced around the room as he dictated, often pausing to examine the globe of the world which stood by the door. That globe is now one of the exhibits at the Longwood museum on St Helena, and I have been told that if you look carefully you can see little scratch marks in the area around the tiny dot of the island, made, so they say, by Napoleon's fingernails.

And so to lunch and a change of clothes and perhaps another ride or a game of chess, and then the mid-point of the day had been reached and it was time for a bath. The bath was an important event, and Chinese and servants worked hard just outside the window of the narrow bathroom, stoking the fire to heat the boiler that would feed a thin trickle of water into the tub. Napoleon sometimes sat in a hot bath for several hours, his head seeming to float on the surface, with books or meals set in front of him on a tray, and someone waiting to talk to him if he felt like talking. More water, more heat, more books, more food, more discussion, and then he would dress in formal clothes, ready to receive any visitor who had come through the cordon of sentries armed with the necessary papers and passwords.

On one occasion in March 1816 a large crowd of officers from a fleet of ships returning from China had been allowed to invade the garden without permission. There were men drifting uneasily among the gum trees and around the house. 'One said that the pride of his life would be that he had seen Napoleon; another that he dare not appear in his wife's presence if he could not tell her that he had been fortunate enough to behold his features.' (Las Cases, vol. I, p. 388) The officers were told that they could enter the house and they stood in a line in the billiard room like soldiers on parade, while Napoleon walked from one to the next, asking questions in French.

Your wife is pretty I hear? How many children have you?

Have you served in India?

Why is your complexion so dark, were you sick?

Do you drink? [and then himself translating the French] Dreenk? Dreenk? (Henry, pp. 18–19)

The interview went on for half an hour and Napoleon's servants kept a watchful eye on all the men to make sure that the Emperor's hat or some other personal possession was not stolen by someone eager to take home a souvenir of the occasion. Always when receiving such afternoon callers Napoleon remained standing so that no one had the presumption of sitting down in his presence. If he was tired he rested his hand on a chair or against the wall.

It was only during the night that he was able to release his tight control of the world around him. At the end of the day he would rush into the rooms of his private 'Interior' like a boxer who had finished a hard fight, 'throwing his hat on the floor, tearing off his coat, the sash of the Legion of Honour, vest, collar, cravat, braces, scattered all around him'. He put on a nightshirt and tied a red Madras handkerchief around his head, and then quickly lay down on one of the little campbeds with their spindly metal legs and their cradle-folds of green curtains. Marchand or St Denis, whichever was on duty, would set a candelabrum with three candles burning beside the bed, and wait in silence while the master began to read a book, threw it on the floor, turned the pages of a newspaper that was already three months old, took another book, changed beds, walked around the room, coughed and said he was cold, then thirsty, then tired. Finally the roar of the wind or the sound of crickets chirping in the darkness would send him to sleep and the waiting servant could remove the candelabrum, light the night-light and settle himself on the carpet. Napoleon usually woke during the night at around one or two in the morning and then there was an anxious search for the return of sleep. He moved over to the other bed, or had the two beds pulled together so that he could stretch himself across both of them or demanded a bath, which meant organising a team of men to light the fire in the darkness outside the window. Often he went to his desk to continue with the account of the life that he had lived, and he would start with the simple thought or event he wished to describe and cross out one word and add another and scribble through whole lines and paragraphs until the workings of his mind were lost in a tangle of scrawls on sheets of paper, and nobody, not even the careful St Denis or Napoleon himself could read in the morning what he had written in the night.

Perhaps it was during one of those hectic hours that Napoleon worked out his strange definition of the two categories of madness, which he explained to Las Cases one day in March 1816. Harmless madmen are those who are unable to make a bridge between ideas and the application of ideas; like a person who eats grapes in a vineyard that does not belong to him and when the rightful owner comes and accuses him of stealing he replies, 'Here are the two of us and the sun shines on us both; therefore I have a right to eat the grapes.' The dangerous madman is someone who cannot understand the division that separates ideas and actions. The example Napoleon gave was of someone who cuts the head off a sleeping man and then conceals himself behind a hedge in order to enjoy the perplexity of the dead body when it wakes up and realises what has happened. Las Cases does not say what might have steered the Emperor's mind towards this strange image, nor whether he felt that he knew many people who belonged to the one or to the other category.

CHAPTER X

A tree is best measured when its down.

English Civil War song

On 14 April 1816 a man called Sir Hudson Lowe arrived at Jamestown with his wife, his children and a collection of personal secretaries, servants and assistants. He had come to take up his recent appointment as governor of the island and guardian of its prisoner. Up until then he had followed a rather obscure career in the secret intelligence section of the British army, and coming to St Helena marked the most important event in his life and the zenith of his public achievements. He was eighteen days younger than Napoleon and he spoke French and Italian fluently, but here the few connecting threads between these two men already begin to snap. Where the one was tall and angular with thin arms and legs, the other was short and round-bellied with plump hands and small feet. Where the one had thick orange hair turning grey and growing in long tufts at his eyebrows and protruding from his nostrils and ears, the other had a curiously naked face with the delicate soft hair of a baby, uniformly brown. Lowe's complexion tended to be fiercely red, although when he was angry it would suddenly turn very pale. Napoleon had a waxy and pallid skin that took on a yellow tinge if he was especially tired or feeling ill, and even sunshine and outdoor exercise produced little change to this pallor, although a single glass of wine could bring a hectic flush to this cheeks.

Several people who worked with Lowe on St Helena or had reason to see him quite regularly have left descriptions of him as he thrashed his way through the doubts and uncertainties that clung to him, avoiding eye contact even when he was talking to someone directly and changing colour like a chameleon as his anger rose and fell. You see him bursting into the room where his private secretary is working, to accuse him of losing some vital piece of paper and then a minute later finding it crumpled up in his own coat pocket. You see him chasing Dr O'Meara down a corridor of Plantation House, shouting abuse after him, and then on the next morning there he is greeting this same doctor in a warm and friendly manner as if the quarrel really had been forgotten. You see him pacing this way and that, his mind always preoccupied with the thought of his prisoner, and slowly his right arm rises up and he presses a finger to his nostril and holds it there, as if this is a way of preventing newly-hatched ideas from escaping before they have been carefully examined. Napoleon took one look at him – this, his destiny cloaked in a human form – and decided that whatever the man's character might prove to be, his face was hideous. 'He looks like a hyena caught in a trap,' he said. Later he elaborated on this description, saying that Lowe had the face of a debt collector, an imbecile, a man only fit to hire assassins, a creature so soaked in evil that just one glance from his malignant eye seemed to poison the cup of coffee that stood on the table between them during one of their brief and tense meetings. 'I have seen Prussians, Tartars, Cossacks, Kalmucks and many others, but never before in my life have I seen so ill-favoured and forbidding a countenance.' (O'Meara (1822), vol. i, p. 54)

In trying to imagine the first meetings that took place between Napoleon the prisoner and Lowe the master of the prison, I cannot help thinking of an account I once read about what happens when a male peacock and a male turkey are placed together. The two birds, bristling with a sense of their own importance, do not realise that they belong to two distinct and unrelated species; instead they see each other as rivals and begin to fight. According to the rules which govern all male peacocks, the one who is losing must save himself by running away and his opponent will never deign to chase him; but according to the rules which govern all male turkeys the loser must lie on the ground with his neck outstretched and by showing his weakness he can be sure of being left unharmed. The turkey is larger but the peacock has the advantage of being much faster, and if they are trapped together in a confined area then their fundamental lack of understanding can lead to bloody and even fatal consequences. In the prison that was St Helena, Napoleon and Lowe strutted and paraded before each other, feathers rippling and colours ablaze, and they managed to weave a strange spell of hatred, insult and wounded pride which held them closely bound together even after they had ceased to fight face to face and only learnt of the other's actions and words from second-hand information. 'We had certainly some reason to complain about the Admiral,' said Napoleon when he had met Lowe a couple of times and the stage was already set between them, 'but at least he was an Englishman. This man is nothing but a cheap Italian debt collector, a *Sbire*. We have not the same manner, we cannot understand each other; our feelings do not speak the same language.' (Las Cases, vol II, p. 237)

The weather was especially bad during the first weeks of April 1816, and the rain and wind were relentless throughout most of the days and nights. On the evening when Lowe was making his initial inspection of Plantation House, the governor's residence that would now be his home, Napoleon was feeling ill and sad and he went to bed early. On the following day Lowe went through the procedure of officially taking over his post and briefly, when the weather cleared, Napoleon went for a walk in the garden accompanied by Las Cases. That same afternoon a messenger arrived from the other side of the island to say that Lowe intended to visit General Bonaparte at nine o'clock the next morning, an hour when Napoleon never considered seeing anyone except those few people who knew him well. That evening he was in a wild good humour, and when the meal was over and he had retired to the drawing-room, he began to talk to his companions in English. Betsy Balcombe had given him a few English lessons while he was staying at the Pavilion and Las Cases had taken over the task during the recent weeks at Longwood, but Napoleon did not find it an easy language to learn. He explained the extent of his difficulties in a letter which he wrote and presented to Las Cases:

Since sixt wek y learn the english and y do not any prgress. Sixt week do fourty and two days. If might have learn fivty word for day, i could know it two thousand and hundred. After this you shall agree that the study one tongue is a great labour. (Quoted in Aubry, p. 190)

Now, with everyone listening attentively, he used his English to tell the story of the French explorer La Pérouse: how he had been shipwrecked, his marvellous and romantic adventures in foreign lands, and his untimely death.

Having managed to kill his hero, step by step in ungrammatical sentences, he burst into sudden and violent laughter: nothing in the entire story was true, he had only wanted to demonstrate how well he was doing in mastering the language of his captors.

The next morning, shortly after nine o'clock and with the rain and the wind as unrelenting as ever, Lowe arrived at Longwood. He was accompanied by the admiral, his complete retinue of servants and a number of soldiers dressed in red. He stood sheltering on the verandah and St Denis came to the door in his costume of green, white and black with gold lace at his neck and wrists. According to one account (Gourgaud's), the entire company was shown into the entrance room, and according to another they were kept waiting outside. St Denis went to inform His Majesty of the visit and returned after a few minutes to say that the Emperor was unwell and could not receive any callers. Lowe was unwilling to leave; he hovered in the entrance room, he hovered on the steps of the verandah and he began to examine the external aspect of the house, scrutinising the walls and windows of the building that contained the man he had come to watch over and who he had not yet seen. While he was doing this Napoleon was fully dressed, standing in his bedroom, gazing at the Governor through the little holes cut in the venetian blinds. As soon as Lowe and his party had passed through the gate leading out of the garden, Napoleon appeared on the verandah. His carriage was brought to him and stepping inside he set off on a fast journey around the inner perimeter of his territory.

It was agreed that the Emperor would meet the Governor at two o'clock on the following afternoon and so at the appointed hour the same group was again assembled on the verandah with the rain still battering down. General Bertrand opened the door and invited them to step through into the anteroom with its smell of paint. Most of

Napoleon's staff were already assembled there, dressed in their full palace livery and lined up stiffly against the walls. The two camps stared at each other but did not speak. After half an hour of waiting in this expectant silence it was announced that the Emperor had entered the drawing-room and was ready to receive the Governor. Lowe went in to meet his prisoner and by accident, or perhaps it was after all by design, the admiral was excluded from this encounter and the door was closed in his face just as he was about to follow.

Lowe opened the conversation in French, but Napoleon asked him to continue in Italian and began with his usual barrage of questions.

'How many years have you been in service?'

'Twenty-eight.'

'Then I am an older soldier than you. I can count almost forty.'

To which Lowe replied, according to his own account of the meeting, 'History, however, will speak of our services in very different ways.' (Aubry, p. 173). In a French version of the conversation his reply was far less defiant and he simply murmured, 'Your years are each so many centuries.' (Gourgaud, p. 48)

Within a few days Lowe had drafted the first of many official reports on the island and its prisoner. He felt that more sentries were needed to keep guard on the house, especially at night. From now on all written communications to and from the inhabitants at Longwood must first go to Plantation House for inspection, and anyone wishing to visit General Bonaparte must obtain a permit signed by Governor Lowe. As it still seemed possible that the prisoner might suddenly slip through the net and disappear, he declared that it was essential for the officer living at Longwood to gain visual proof of Napoleon's existence, twice every day.

Lowe also had some suggestions to make with regard to

the house itself. He had noticed that its special defect was what he called its 'scattered style of buildings and its lack of any enclosed areas'. To remedy this problem he suggested that

> a considerable quantity of iron railing be sent out by some of the first ships from England, sufficient to enclose a space of at least 600 yards. To make other enclosures and divisions it might be advisable to send out about 1,200 yards of invisible fence, or a somewhat closer construction than is ordinarily used. (Forsyth, pp. 151–2)

Lowe had already demanded that Napoleon's close companions should sign a declaration that they would stay on the island for as long as their leader was there, and then on 27 April he arrived unexpectedly at Longwood and demanded that all of Napoleon's servants be brought before him to swear that they had come here of their own free will. While this was being done, with Napoleon lurking out of sight in his 'Interior' and Las Cases in attendance, Lowe remarked conversationally on what a beautiful location the house had, such a commanding aspect, such fine and open views of the landscape all around. Las Cases replied that he wished there were a few trees here since the garden became so fierce and arid in the sunlight, and Lowe responded with great confidence, 'Oh, we will plant some,' as if a tree was like a fence or a building, that could be sent for from England and erected fully grown and flourishing in a new location. (Las Cases, vol. II, p. 101)

Before leaving, Lowe paused to walk around the house several times, measuring the height of windows, the length of walls, the distance from a fence to an outbuilding, from an outbuilding to a gate. He explained to Dr O'Meara that the garden was in need of a series of new ditches to make sure that no cattle ever trespassed on the property. There were some old ditches there already, but they were not deep enough or high enough to inspire confidence. He came to a place where the branches of a gum tree trailed over the intersection between two of these old ditches, and staring at it with a look of 'gathering fear' he ordered it to be grubbed out as soon as possible. For the next two months teams of soldiers and Chinese were set to work digging ditches and building palisades, and the occupants of Longwood watched as chunks of turf from the garden were cut away to be used to bank up these mushrooming fortifications. People began to refer to Longwood house as Hudson Fort, and it was reported to Las Cases that the Governor would sometimes start abruptly out of his sleep, struck by inspiration for a new detail to add to his labyrinth of security.

On the evening after Lowe had come to question the servants about their loyalty and to make plans to protect the house from stray cattle, Napoleon had taken on the task of trying to work out exactly what mistakes he had made at the Battle of Waterloo: the details of actions and decisions that had served to divert his destiny to this island. The next day he stayed in his room reading and gave orders that he did not wish to be disturbed. Captain Poppleton was obliged to inform the Governor of the difficulty he now had in fulfilling his duty of catching sight of the prisoner on two occasions every twenty-four hours: 'He did not quit his apartment even to dinner. I ascertained his being there in the morning by the usual ringing of his bell.' (Lowe Papers, 20,208)

Napoleon was still confined to his room on 30 April when Lowe decided to pay him an unexpected visit in the afternoon. He asked if he might be granted an audience, and was told that he could.

I passed through his dining room, drawing room, another room in which were displayed a great number of maps and plans laid out on a table and several loose quires of writing, apparently memoirs and extracts, and was then introduced into an inner apartment with a small bed in it and a couch, on which latter Bonaparte was reclining, having only his dressing gown and without his shoes. His countenance was unusually sallow and even bloated. (Lowe Papers, 20,133)

So there was Napoleon lying in a white coat on a white couch with books scattered on the floor all around him and a two-day growth of beard giving his face its haggard expression. He waved the Governor to a nearby chair and without waiting to learn the reason for this visit began to complain about the predicament he was in.

This island is too small for me. The climate is not like ours, it is not our sun, nor does it have our seasons. Everything breathes a mortal boredom here. The situation is disagreeable, unhealthy. There is no water. This part of the island is a desert. It has chased all its inhabitants away. (Las Cases, vol. II, p. 117)

Lowe answered that he was only obeying instructions and doing what was required of him, and in order to shift the direction of the conversation he began to talk about a new house, a wooden palace which had been specially made by the British government for Napoleon and that was already at this moment somewhere on the Atlantic Ocean and approaching closer to the island each day: a vast toy that should help to amuse a child lying sick and helpless in his bed. Napoleon said he was not the slightest bit interested in the latest news of his wooden palace; what he wanted was newspapers that were not three months old, news of his family, more books to read. He did not need a house filled with furniture; he needed an executioner and a coffin. In the growing darkness of his bedroom he tried to stare at the features of the man he was speaking to, to see if any of his words were taking root.

Napoleon remained within his 'Interior' for several more days, sitting or lying in a shuttered room with the curtains drawn and the blinds pulled down so that no sentry or British officer could peer in on him. Outside the rain still clattered down. He said that there was little to distinguish the days from the nights except that the nights seemed longer. When he stood up his legs were too weak to hold him and when he walked from one corner of the room to the other like an animal in its cage the effort exhausted him and he needed to rest again.

Then on 5 May he broke his own pattern of seclusion as abruptly as he had made it. He went for a ride in the morning, talked with guests who had stopped at the island on their way back from China during the day and with Las Cases in the evening. A fire was lit in his bedroom and since he did not want any candles they sat together in the flickering darkness until eight o'clock when he announced that he wished to be alone. On the next day, with the weather much quieter, he went out into the garden and continued with his study of the Battle of Waterloo until he felt that he could pinpoint the few genuine errors he had made.

On 7 May an English ship arrived at Jamestown harbour bringing with it Napoleon's wooden palace, packed into wooden crates like a vast and inscrutable jigsaw puzzle. The furniture and fittings for this building had been designed by the famous cabinet-maker Mr George Bullock and made up according to his specifications at Woolwich in London. The English newspapers were filled with reports about the taste, the splendour and the regal dignity that was embodied in Napoleon's future home. The front was in the Grecian style with fourteen fine windows on the ground floor, and the building in its entirety stretched to a length of one hundred and twenty feet and contained forty rooms, all of excellent proportions. Amongst the many items of furniture there was a bath lined with marble, a canopy bedstead with draperies in lilac and gold, a book-case in the Etruscan style, a table of veined British oak, Greek sofas and footstools, and a bronze wine cooler that was shaped like a Greek Bacchanalian vase. There were also four hundred packages of what was called stationery: wallpaper for the drawing-room in light tints of sage green with ornamental panels in Arabesque gold, curtains of Pomona green bordered with green velvet and edged with gold-coloured silken twist. The carpets and wallhangings for the dining-room were lavender 'falling into blues', while the sitting-room was to be done with 'ethereal blue intermingled with black' (*Morning Chronicle*, 25 October 1815).

The crates containing the palace and its contents were unloaded and deposited at a warehouse in Jamestown awaiting further instructions. It was said by some of the men who managed to take a look inside them that they seemed to contain 'nothing but a number of rough planks, which no one knows how to put together at St Helena, and which it would take several years to fit up'. (Las Cases, vol. II, pp. 136–7) The same ship also brought Lowe's special consignment of fencing and railings which was put into storage, waiting for the moment when it could be placed in position.

CHAPTER XI

There is nothing either good or bad,
but thinking makes it so.

Shakespeare, *Hamlet*

It is May 1990 and for the last few weeks it has seemed as if this was already midsummer with the sky silent and uniformly blue and the air dry even though the leaves on the trees are only just emerging, cautiously unwrapping themselves, burnt at their soft edges. In less than two months we shall be on the boat that will take us to St Helena: myself, my husband and our two children, packed into a four-berth cabin with air-conditioning to help us ignore the gathering heat as we travel south and a porthole through which we can watch the movement of the ocean as we pass down between the continents of Africa and South America, with no sight of land for the two thousand miles between the Canary Islands and the white tip of Ascension.

We have a map of the depths of the oceans pinned to a

cupboard door in the kitchen and every day I look briefly at the landscape over which we shall be travelling. It is strange to imagine crossing over such a vast area and seeing nothing of its mountains and valleys, its creatures and vegetation, except when a flying fish or a dolphin bursts through the surface or a knot of weed bobs behind in the ship's wake. For some days our route will take us directly above a shadowed underwater silhouette which echoes the shape of Africa and seems to be the unmistakable scar that was left behind when it pulled away from the continent of America. Near that scar there are deep cracks in the sea-bed which are so close to the molten heart of the earth's core that the water there is permeated with an unnatural heat. I read something recently about the great worm-like creatures that have been detected in such cracks, and photographed as dim white tubes moving and rolling in a heavy darkness where nothing should be able to live or find sustenance. Halfway through our journey, with Georgetown in Guyana on our right and Freetown in the Gambia on our left, we go through the Doldrum Fracture Zone where there is sometimes no movement of wind or water for weeks on end and where once sailors would contemplate a mirage of their own despair. I have been led to believe that every evening a little band will play for the entertainment of the guests on board, although even as I write this it suddenly seems rather unlikely and I can't remember where I got the information from. And every day the little swimming pool will tip and tilt with the movement of the waves beneath us.

The ship could be carrying as many as one hundred and thirty passengers, as well as letters and parcels, packets of Cornflakes and jars of Marmite and other essentials or luxuries that the inhabitants of St Helena have called for. Since we won't be staying in a hotel we have been advised to take a supply of food with us, but I have still not found out what sort of food would be best. I have met one women who will be travelling on this same crossing and she is bringing a spare tyre for her brother's car. She was born on the island and is a schoolteacher and a respected figure in the church. When I met her she was wearing a daffodil yellow suit with a white blouse, white shoes and a white handbag; by way of a greeting she gave me a thin-armed, cool-skinned hug. There will also be a botanist on board, an Italian I think he is, who has written a paper about the island's vegetation and now wants to make sure retrospectively that he has not made any mistakes.

The journey should take sixteen days, which will leave us almost four weeks on the island before we set off again back the same way that we have come. I hope that during those weeks I can find people who will talk to me about Fernando Lopez and Napoleon, about goats and rats and the weather, about the past and the present and the way of life that they have grown accustomed to. I know that I must be very careful in what I say and what I do not say; there is a hierarchy of colour and class on the island and there is still a sharp division between those who support Napoleon and those who dislike everything that is associated with his memory. Longwood, and its bleak garden, the Vale of Geranium and its empty grave, the Pavilion and what was once the garden at The Briars, these little patches of land belong to the French, while the rest of St Helena is an English dominion, one of the last fragments of empire. The French Consul, who lives at Longwood and has done so for the last thirty years, does not have a great deal to do with the English Governor who lives at Plantation House but only took up his post some months ago.

The people of Jamestown have very different manners and customs to the inland people, and those in the east are nothing like those in the south or the west. The older generation turn their backs on the modern world, but the young men and women often curse the place they have been born in because it allows them so little freedom of movement or choice. I read a book recently in which the author said that the atmosphere on St Helena reminded him very specifically of the atmosphere in the sacred city of Delphi, where the temple was dedicated to the ambiguity of all life and where a white stone tied with a red ribbon marked the navel of the world. Perhaps, once I have been there, I will understand what he means.

Several months ago I wrote a letter to the Governor, but the British Foreign Office gave me the name of his predecessor and I never received a reply. Then I wrote to the archivist at the museum in Jamestown and he advised me not to visit the island, saying that there was nothing in the collection that was not also held by the Public Records Office Library in London. I was later told that it was unwise of me to have mentioned the name Napoleon, that was bound to have irritated him. I wrote to the French Consul at Longwood, and he never replied either, although I did speak to him on the telephone while he was in France for the celebration of the bicentenary of the storming of the Bastille and the Revolution. I have been informed by two different sources that the Consul's clothes are made of mohair and silk and that he often hears the ghosts of the Emperor and his companions arguing in the rooms around him, but I wonder if he will want to talk to me about this. I sometimes imagine myself walking up the elegant drive that leads to Plantation House, the building still the same dove grey and white, and inside the wallpaper on the walls, the carpets on the floor, the furniture and the uniforms of the officials all unchanged since the days when Sir Hudson Lowe stalked along the corridors, his mind preoccupied with his prisoner. I imagine myself walking across Deadwood Plain with the low outline of Longwood approaching closer and the Consul looking like the one photograph I have seen of him, bearded and immaculately dressed in white, standing in the garden that is now maintained as a French monument.

I once spent a year on an island. It was very different to the one I am now going to: it was large and Mediterranean and served by an airport which brought in thousands, maybe even millions of tourists during the high season. I first arrived at the end of the summer and as the weather began to change and the visitors to leave there was a sense of the air evaporating, bringing those of us who remained into an uneasy closeness, even though we were mostly strangers to each other. There were newspapers and radio and television, and people went to the mainland or elsewhere quite regularly and returned smelling of the outside world, but still there was the sense that the only important reality was the details of daily life in this little village, with a ring of high mountains at its back and a steep track down to the coast: two shops, three cafés and a bus that thundered along the main street twice a day. Every domestic quarrel or infidelity, a party or a hangover, all travelled from house to house, settled and moved on like a flock of chattering birds. For the sake of talk or entertainment the most extraordinary casual malice would erupt briefly and then disappear leaving almost no trace. At the centre of this curious hubbub there was the presence of Robert Graves, who was by then already growing increasingly remote, but who still dominated the village by the simple fact of his existence and the acclaim that he had once won for himself. If someone visited him at his home and saw him there, vast and impassive, then the meeting would be talked about and compared with other meetings until it acquired a vividness and a significance in its amputated state that it could never have had at its first moment. But then the winter months moved on, and the atmosphere was again diluted by the spring and the arrival of new faces, and the intensity of gossip and scandal was dispersed and mostly forgotten.

Now if a crowded Mediterranean village makes a claustrophobic home for a single winter, and if a chance visitor to St Helena like myself has already been warned half a dozen times about what to say and what not to say and how to circumnavigate the danger of sudden insult or anger, then what must it have been like on that distant island in Napoleon's time, with the first year of his captivity drawing to a close and the second year grinding into motion? When you read the books, the journals and the letters written by people who were there, you cannot avoid the impression that all of them, even the most calm and reasonable individuals, seem to be speaking through clenched teeth. With nothing to do and nothing to be done and the rest of the world so far away, the island was bound to become saturated in an atmosphere of intrigue and mistrust, fear and rage, that spread among the human population like the contagion of a disease. It was not simply a case of Napoleon and his supporters colliding with the English and their network of power; the betrayals and the backbiting could be found everywhere, among friends as well as among strangers and newly-made enemies.

Napoleon, talking to Las Cases in May 1817, said that he thought it was always a mistake to presume on knowing a person's character. Just as it was impossible to judge a man's soul by looking at his face, so too it was impossible to know how someone would behave in certain situations; human beings were not predictable, and in a crisis they tended to react mysteriously and unthinkingly. He had learnt this from watching men on the battlefield and now he was learning it again watching himself and the others on the island.

People who have written about the extended season of Napoleon's captivity usually presume on the logic and predictability of human actions. At the outset they tend to take sides, and once they have established themselves either in the French or the English camp, they go on to try to prove that this man told lies and therefore is not to be trusted in anything that he said; that one was mad, while that one was plotting to murder the Emperor from the very first day he arrived. In proving their arguments they gather up all the evidence that has been left by the people who were there; they check diaries against letters and published writing and attempt to strip a man or a woman into a nakedness where nothing can be hidden, or produce a few battered fragments that can perhaps be called the truth. Somehow this process makes me think of the later stripping of the body of Napoleon and the strident claims that this is a genuine lock of his hair, this a piece of his rib, this his penis. But perhaps instead it can be accepted that the circumstances in which the people on St Helena lived were so odd and unnatural that everyone behaved out of character and contradicted even their own expectations of themselves.

I am sure that it is true that the Irish doctor, Barry O'Meara, who was Napoleon's personal doctor and close advisor for the first two years, also sometimes acted as Lowe's spy, and betrayed each side to the other as he moved from Longwood to Plantation House and back again. But that does not invalidate the book he wrote later, which condemned the way that Napoleon was treated, nor does it make him into a liar. I am sure that it is true that the diminutive and worried figure of Las Cases, his eyesight and his health failing him and everyone mocking him for the way that he worshipped the man who had once been emperor, exaggerated the conditions at Longwood, the heat and the rats, the rotten food and the insults, as well as the fine phrases dropped from the mouth of Napoleon. But Las Cases in his little room, stifling in the sunshine, damp when it rained, with the Emperor so close he could hear him breathing, and a fear of death and absurdity always close to him, was sincere in his interpretation of the situation and he certainly did not write his book just to insult the English. Perhaps Montholon did poison Napoleon with careful doses of arsenic at the end, but he was a dedicated companion until that end and one of the few who survived the entire length of the captivity. And anyway after all those years Napoleon longed to die, so it could have been a kindness and not a betrayal. Even Sir Hudson Lowe was possibly an honest and good-natured man, but haunted day and night by the responsibility of having to guard Napoleon until his prisoner seemed to be always waiting somewhere close to him, like a malevolent genie sprung from a bottle.

It could be said that there were simply too many people confined on a small island for an apparently unlimited length of time, and that was in itself a nightmare. The islanders had never been self-sufficient, but with the sudden arrival of even more regulations to circumscribe them and an army of soldiers, sailors and officials in need of food and drink, they hid under a blanket of passivity and gave up almost every attempt to cultivate the land or raise livestock. This meant that all their food, and other essential supplies, had to be imported. Coal arrived from New-castle, cattle made the rough crossing from Angola, two hundred thousand gallons of Cape wine were ordered in a single year and two thousand pounds of barley were consumed each day. Again and again the supply of fresh meat, of writing paper, coal or candles, sugar or coffee, would suddenly run out, and then it could take months for a new consignment to make its slow way across the ocean, through storms, doldrums and official bureaucracy.

After a few months at Longwood there was no more writing paper to be found anywhere on the island, a loss which horrified Las Cases; the eau-de-Cologne ran out and Napoleon had to accept being rubbed down with lavender water; then a consignment of wine was sour and gave everyone piercing headaches, and the only vegetable available was potatoes. When a supply ship did arrive at Jamestown it was often found to contain dying cattle, or sheep from the Cape with fat tails and thin carcasses, or rotting vegetables, or a load of candles which had been ordered because they were cheap but which were so badly made that they dripped themselves into a pool of wax within half an hour of being lit. One writer who had no reason to exaggerate declared that 'all of the produce is of bad quality and in quantity never more than the bare minimum. Half of it is not fit to be eaten.' Even when the goods were not damaged on arrival, there was the problem of storing them, and it was said by some that Lowe was too busy preparing for battle to find the time to build a storehouse, and so the goods were often left unattended in their crates, presumably in the company of some of the crates that contained sections of Napoleon's wooden palace, his marble bath and his fine silk wallhangings.

It is easy to see how such simple material irritations drove people mad, while the weather, according to several diaries, was so bad that it made them depressed even before they got up in the morning. There are various accounts of the rats at Longwood, but everyone agrees that they were numerous and O'Meara described how they would hold competitions to see how many could be killed in the dining-room during a single evening. He also described how they would mill about in the daytime outside the kitchen, and how once a rat jumped out of Napoleon's hat when he was about to put it on after dinner. In a short book she wrote about her years on the island, Madame de Montholon tells how the bedbugs hid in the satin sheets and in the bedhangings which were intended to keep out the mosquitoes, and how a particularly vicious fly hovered around the gum trees in the garden and attacked anyone who went out walking or riding. Although Longwood looked quite clean when it was first occupied, by the end of the first year the damp and the heat caused the tar on the roof to bubble so that the ceilings leaked when it rained, and the wallpaper was black with patches of mould. The curtains and carpets were also affected by the damp and the silk dresses of the ladies were damaged. Napoleon complained that the white curtains in his bedroom were filthy and since he was not provided with any spare ones he hung bed sheets up instead. Water had to be brought in a bucket from a spring that was almost half a mile away and when it arrived it was warm and, according to O'Meara, thick.

Napoleon had another meeting with Sir Hudson Lowe on 16 May. The Governor was again interested in where 'New Longwood' should be sited and in which items of furniture Napoleon wished to have the use of in the meantime. Napoleon was so angry that the muscles in the calf of his left leg began to vibrate, a sure sign which he had experienced before. There was another brief and unsuccessful meeting in June, from which Lowe went away saying that Napoleon, having created an imaginery Spain, France and Poland, was now busy creating an imaginary St Helena. When he was told of this Napoleon laughed and said that the Governor was going to kill him.

On 20 August, three days after Napoleon's forty-seventh birthday, the two men had their last encounter. They met in the garden in the presence of the English Admiral Sir Pulteney Malcolm and Napoleon made a point of insulting Lowe to his face in front of his fellow officer, calling him a liar and a cheat. Shortly afterwards Lowe began to make arrangements to reduce the spending at Longwood; table salt was one of the many items that he felt was being used much too freely.

CHAPTER XII

Men must endure
Their going hence even as their coming
    hither:
Ripeness is all.

Shakespeare, *King Lear*

For the sake of establishing a clear separation between time
past and time present, I feel that I must have Napoleon
dead and buried before we begin to make our way towards
his island. Or, if not buried, then at least at the point where
he is lying on his military campbed in the drawing-room at
Longwood, with the venetian blinds pulled down and all
those of his servants and companions who are still with
him taking it in turns to stand beside him and stare at the
lifeless face of a man who had been an emperor.

I don't quite understand this sense of urgency, but it is as
if, once I have reached the island, I will be entering the
second stage of the story; the thread that I have been
following up until now will be broken and there will be no
way to reconnect it. I realise that I have reached only the
end of 1816 and there are almost four years waiting to be

accounted for and in a few more weeks we will be on the boat. Still I can try to work my way through those years as quickly as possible, and then even if I cannot let Napoleon die in time for our departure, at least I can bring him to the brink of his death, and perhaps if the weather remains calm as we journey down the South Atlantic, I can begin to describe his end before we reach St Helena. It should not take more than one chapter to explain how it was that Las Cases and Gourgaud, O'Meara and the Balcombe family, along with several others who had meant to stay, all left the island and what changes their departure brought about. The next visible landmark is a brief eruption of energy that concentrated itself around the making of a garden at Longwood and the shift in the balance of the household that was caused by the arrival of two priests, a doctor and a servant from Europe. After that there is nothing more to be seen except the gradual and inexorable movement towards death. Within each chapter the weather, the supply of food and provisions, people's health and conversation and whatever other details seem to claim attention, can emerge and sink back again into the books, the diaries and the letters from which they have come, and after three chapters I can see nothing to stop me from entering that room where Napoleon lies on his thin-legged metal bed, dressed for the occasion in all the medals and fine silks of his rank and military status.

And when those silent people stand around him, I think I can presume that all of them are trying to wipe out every recollection of the ridiculous monotony of the daily life that they have been living for so long, so that they can concentrate their minds on the significance of what they are now witnessing. They, just like Napoleon himself, have been doing nothing much else for the last years besides waiting for this moment, and now that it has come they must absorb it with great care; let it seep into their skins like music or strong sunlight.

I can remember sitting beside the bed of my stepmother when she was on the edge of death after a long illness. Sitting there holding her paper-skinned hand and trying to say goodbye, I was sometimes able to be with her in that white quiet, but sometimes I could only look in and see the two of us from what seemed like a far distance, while all around me the air was filled with the loud chattering of all the images and memories connected with this particular person I had known so well. And there is a second fragmented reflection which appears before me now, demanding to be seen. It is that of Robert Graves, who in certain ways closely resembled my idea of an emperor. I was staying as a guest in his house and there was a night on which I was woken by the sound of his crying out in his sleep and I went into his room with his wife and saw him thrashing on his bed in a strange and distant agony. After a few moments it was over, and his breathing was peaceful again, but many times since then I have found my mind watching that event: a little loop of film which plays before my eyes and shows an old man practising the difficult task of letting go of life, shaking it away from him.

With the gradual tightening of the constraints that hemmed him in from all sides, it seems as if Napoleon had no choice but to learn how to die. He always had a very slow pulse rate and used to say to his doctors that he doubted if he had a heart at all since he had never heard it or felt it beating; but this metabolism that must have kept him unperturbed in the clamour of battle and activity, made him heavy and listless once the fighting was over. It was as if he had raced so fast all his life that now he had to sit still and wait for his destiny to catch up with him and do what it liked in disposing of him.

Towards the end of 1816 Sir Hudson Lowe received clear instructions from London telling him that he must economise on the running costs of Longwood, but he need spare no expense in preventing his prisoner from escaping.

He decided that Napoleon needed to be even more closely supervised than before, and he ordered that from now on the prisoner could only ride on horseback within an eight-mile circumference of the house and if he wanted to go further then he must be accompanied by an English officer. Napoleon had been in the habit of riding out quite regularly, often with Gourgaud, and the two of them took air guns to shoot at partridges or pigeons, while the Emperor filled his pockets with gold coins embossed with his own head so that he could throw one to a slave who opened a gate for him, or offer one to a soldier who saluted or an islander whose face happened to please him. Sometimes he would hurtle carelessly through fences and into the gardens of strangers, and then stop and talk with whoever came out to meet him. But now, within the new limits of his freedom, an officer had to be always there beside him, watching and listening, and so Napoleon stopped going riding and made less and less use of his body. Anger and despair combined with the rain and the wind to keep him in the house for days on end and he would fall ill from his own enforced inactivity as well as from the other complaints that were native to his body; so he had headaches and toothaches, dizziness, insomnia and a pain in the region of his liver, while his belly grew fatter and his legs had a tendency to swell. He would move from bed to sofa to the bath that turned his skin pink with the heat of the water, and his trail was marked by a scattering of books and newspapers, while his servants and anyone else who thought themselves able to please him, hovered around, trying to encourage him back into the world. On the occasions when he did go outside he could be seen tottering around the garden in flimsy decorative shoes that got wet in the puddles, or sitting lost in a blur of thoughts as he gazed at the horizon, the soldiers, the clouds, the outline of the mountains.

In September 1816 Napoleon had called O'Meara to him

and asked, 'Doctor, can you give sleep to a man who cannot sleep? I have been trying in vain to procure a little rest.' (O'Meara (1822), vol. 1, p. 114) As the pattern of the years began to establish itself, the passivity of the days was counteracted by the restlessness of the nights, and even when Napoleon did manage to sleep then his dreams were more exhausting than his wakefulness. He sometimes mentioned these dreams, but only their subject, not the direction in which they had taken him. There were many occasions when he would wake up and announce, 'I dreamt of Paris.'

A crate of books is delivered unexpectedly, and he is so eager to see what has been brought to him that in the middle of the night he cracks the lid off with a chisel and reads almost without a pause for several days until he is exhausted. An ice-making machine arrives and everyone gathers round to watch it transform a glass of water into a lump of ice. The dampness of the days makes it necessary to dry the playing cards in the oven before they can be used and the piano has gone hopelessly out of tune. Santini, a Corsican whose duties include cutting Napoleon's hair and making new linings for his hats, goes out at night hunting for wild pigs on Deadwood Plain and everyone says that if he happens to meet Sir Hudson Lowe in the darkness he will not hesitate to shoot him. Montholon becomes convinced that the house has a ghost who creeps around its walls trying to get in, and he complains to Napoleon that he is also being kept awake at night by the sound of so many of the servants copulating with their mistresses, their new wives or the black prostitutes who can be hired in Jamestown. Napoleon tells him to stop fussing, this place is not a convent and how else are people supposed to entertain themselves? Las Cases, frightened by his failing eyesight, falls ill with hepatitis and his son develops a heart disease which makes him shake and sweat. Gourgaud has a severe bout of dysentery and nearly dies; Bertrand sprains his ankle and cannot walk; Madame Montholon wears very low-cut dresses and says that the island is ageing her prematurely, while Madame Bertrand is pregnant and unhappy. Napoleon tells the two ladies that when they put on their evening gowns and their jewellery, they look like a couple of peasant women dressed up in their Sunday best and Madame Bertrand is so insulted that she avoids coming to Longwood, while Madame Montholon persists in being endlessly talkative and artificially charming so that O'Meara declares that he can't stand the sight of her.

As part of the attempt to economise on household expenses Lowe demands the dismissal of four of Napoleon's servants. It is decided that Santini the haircutter must go, along with Rousseau the lamplighter (who had made the pretty carriage drawn by a team of mice), Archambault who helped his brother with the horses, and a Polish gentleman called Pienkowski whom nobody liked and who seemed to have no clear duties. Then in the following month Las Cases is arrested and is taken along with his son to the Castle prison in Jamestown before being deported to Europe. He is accused of trying to smuggle two letters written on silk out of the island and all his personal papers are seized including the enormous diary that he saw as the cord that would bind his name with Napoleon's for ever. The removal of this earnest and obsequious gentleman changes the pecking order in the Longwood household; whereas Montholon and Gourgaud had previously been united in their dislike for Las Cases, they now turn their resentments against each other. Napoleon spends a great deal of time in his room, he has lost the desire to dictate his memoirs and he rarely bothers to get dressed. On the eve of the new year of 1817 he announces ominously that he feels as if he is living in a tomb.

But life goes on. Marchand and St Denis rub Napoleon down with lavender water and he gazes in the mirror at his white rounded arms, his softly swelling breasts on a white and hairless chest and says, 'Look, would I not make a beautiful woman with breasts like these?' Madame Bertrand gives birth to a boy in January 1817, and Madame Montholon's little daughter Napolienne, who is said to have a broad heavy chin resembling the Emperor's, cuts her first teeth and cries incessantly. When he is in a good humour Napoleon tries to encourage every member of his 'family' to be merry and contented, in spite of the circumstances that surround them. 'If your daughter cries, then you must sing to her,' he tells Madame Montholon, and he begins with the first verse of a nursery rhyme:

> My father is at home,
> What do you want to do?
> What *do* you want to do?

With Las Cases removed from the island it is no longer possible to rely on his fastidious account of each important event and every conversation in which his master took part. Gourgaud keeps a diary, but it is a very different version of events: he describes dancing with a woman who first treads on his foot and then farts; he discusses the cost of whores in Jamestown and he complains bitterly about his wasted life, the boredom he has to suffer, the unpleasant weather and Napoleon's lack of appreciation of him. Napoleon mutters that this puppy loves him like a woman, but he is not a woman, he has not a woman's cunt and all he wishes for is to be left alone.

Nevertheless, Dr Gourgaud's diary, together with Dr O'Meara's and accounts written by the others who were on the island, can be pieced together to give a sense of the slow passing of time at Longwood. One day Napoleon asks Gourgaud to help him dismantle his campbed because he wants to know how heavy it is, and the exact measurements of its legs and its sides. On another day he asks for the Imperial Almanac to be brought to him so that he can look up the population of Amsterdam, the age of his brothers, the names of all the ladies who once waited on him at court: 'Ah it was a pretty Empire! I had eighty-three million human beings to govern!' (Gourgaud, p. 121) He goes to Marchand's room under the hot roof of the attic, and there he peers into the mahogany wardrobe in which hangs the coat of the First Consul, the blue cloak from the Battle of Marengo, a grey frock coat, a green one, scarves and laces: 'What, so many of my things still here?'

The arrival of a bundle of old newspapers fills him with enthusiasm until he has read them all and is again back in the present moment. In a good humour he talks about how he would have liked to live in the countryside, somewhere in Europe 'where a sick sheep makes a subject for conversation'. Or in Paris, living on twelve francs a day and dining on thirty sous; going to libraries and literary salons and taking a cheap seat at the theatre every evening. Or putting on a disguise and travelling through the country: 'If ever I get to England I shall go travelling there in that way'. (Gourgaud, in Aubry, p. 324)

The time of the evening meal is to be changed; now it will take place at three in the afternoon, then at two, then back to three and slowly it returns to its original hour. The work on the memoirs is mostly forgotten and often instead of reading Napoleon calls for his snuff-boxes or a set of maps to be brought to him, so that he can look at them. The two older children of Bertrand and Montholon run wild through the house, but although there is talk of giving them lessons, nothing is done. Napoleon spends an increasing amount of time in the company of his servants and Cipriani, the maître d'hôtel, confides to O'Meara that his master is losing his wits: 'It all began with Waterloo and now he's beginning to believe in God.'

On his forty-eighth birthday Napoleon appears dressed in an old green hunting coat that has been 'turned' to hide its worn appearance. Even for this occasion he does not wear his three-cornered hat, saying that he is reserving it 'for great occasions' (Aubry, p. 329), and he never wears it again, although it is placed in his coffin with him. He repeatedly apologises for being alive at all, and like an unwelcome guest who promises he will soon go home he reassures his servants and companions that he expects to be dead within a year. When Gourgaud is unhappy about seeing so little of His Majesty he is told that he can expect to inherit a fifth of Napoleon's wealth. 'By staying here you can make yourself famous. Besides I shall not live long and I can make your fortune.' (Gourgaud, in Aubry, p. 313)

By the middle of 1817 Napoleon has decided that he wants no more English visitors to come to Longwood, neither the eager crowds of silent tourists nor the occasional person of importance who would like to come and talk with him. But in August of that year he does accept a visit from Captain Basil Hall, who is returning to England after a long stay in China. This man's father had been a fellow student of Napoleon's at the military academy at Brienne, 'the first Englishman I ever met', and filled with distant memories he talks to the son about China and about an island called Loo Tchoo in the China Seas where the people know nothing of wars or money. 'They know nothing of Europe,' Hall tells him. 'They do not know of France or England. They haven't heard of Your Majesty.' (Basil Hall, in Aubry, p. 332)

In September 1817 Gourgaud goes to Plantation House weeping like a child and he begs Lowe to give him permission to leave St Helena. He says, 'I see His Majesty only a quarter of an hour a day and then just to watch a game of chess, put the pieces away, or snuff out the candles.' (Gourgaud, in Aubry, p. 338) He says that he has been treated 'like a dog' and he leaves the island in a thick tangle of blame and recrimination, although after he has been back to Europe for a year he grows quiet again and his adulation for the Emperor returns. On the same boat that takes Gourgaud, are the Balcombe family, under a cloud of suspicion because Mr Balcombe is thought to have tried to smuggle letters out of Longwood.

Napoleon appears to be untroubled by these departures but when a short time later Cipriani falls ill and is dead within three days, nothing can quieten his grief and people watch as he paces this way and that, unable to stand still or sit down even for a moment.

During the first months of 1818 Napoleon spends a lot of time with Dr O'Meara, but then he is accused of spying and is ordered to leave the island and after that it is as if no one can stand the strain at Longwood and everyone wants to get away. Pierron the pastrycook and St Denis the man-servant present themselves at Plantation House and ask if they can go; Madame Bertrand begs Napoleon to release her husband from his duties for a year; Madame Montholon obtains a doctor's certificate which declares that the state of her liver and stomach and the exhaustion caused by a recent miscarriage make it imperative that she obtain proper medical attention as soon as possible. Napoleon fights hard to persuade the last of his companions to stay with him; he promises that he will soon be dead and draws up a first draft of his will to show how much money will be theirs once he has gone. The Bertrands agree to comply with his wishes, and so do the servants and Montholon, but in July 1818 Madame Montholon boards a boat for Europe, and her husband is caught in a downpour on his way back from seeing her off and is confined to his bed for several weeks with bronchitis and rheumatism.

By now the only person keeping a record of what is going on at Longwood is Captain George Nicholls, the new Orderly Officer who has the difficult task of catching sight of Napoleon twice a day and making a report to the Governor on the prisoner's apparent state of health. He writes a letter to Lowe in which he says that his own health will soon be in danger if, in spite of the weather, 'I am under the necessity of continuing the system of walking around Longwood House in the execution of my duty'. He asks if the *sound* of Napoleon would not serve just as well as a proof of his existence as the sight of him: 'I believe I heard him today, singing or humming a tune . . . I distinctly heard his bell.' (Lowe Papers, 20,210) But Lowe is adamant that the prisoner must be seen, and tells his personal secretary that he himself 'would have a hole bored through the ceiling if [Bonaparte] would not show himself, and set people there to peep through and watch him. He proposed to [Captain Nicholls] to sneak about the windows in the evening and put his ears to crevices and peep through shutters and afterwards told me how odd it was that people seemed to conceive these things as a matter of delicacy.' (Kemble/Gorrequer, p. 94)

Napoleon did put a great deal of effort into avoiding being seen. He would hide in his bedroom with the blind drawn and then walk out into the garden the moment he knew that Nicholls was busy elsewhere. After he had managed to be consistently out of sight for two days Lowe gave orders for the door to his private apartments to be forced open, and Napoleon reacted by having all the doors and windows barricaded against such an attack. He slept with a gun next to his bed, while St Denis was in the dining-room armed with another gun and Marchand guarded the bathroom and Noverraz was in the kitchen.

On 14 August, three days before Napoleon's forty-ninth birthday, Nicholls was standing in the garden and peering hopefully through the shutters of the bathroom window when suddenly the Emperor rose up out of the bath in which he had been lying for more than two hours, and white-skinned, naked and wet he walked up to the shuttered window and stood there so that he could be clearly seen.

CHAPTER XIII

Fortune and misfortune have no fixed
    abode
This one and the other are given us in
    turn.
Shao P'in working in his field of
    melons
Was much as he had been when Lord
    of Tung Ling province.

                T'ao Ch'ien, 365–427 AD

In July 1819, with so many people gone from Longwood and no more visitors coming to the house to demand attention and disturb the repetition of the days, Napoleon drew up the first plans for the making of a garden: an outer shell to his prison that would give him places where he could hide from the eyes of the sentries and from the battering of the wind; avenues of tall trees where he could walk in the shade; a summerhouse where he could take tea and a grotto where breakfast could be served; a pool for golden carp, a cage for singing birds, a fountain of delicately cascading water.

Ever since starting this story I have been looking forward to this stage of its development, but now that I have reached it I find my thoughts scattering, breaking up into a kaleidoscope of images, making it difficult to focus on a fixed centre. Near to where I live there is a sea cliff of sand and gravel and fine grey earth, and whenever the tide is high and the waves are especially fierce, then chunks of this cliff are broken off like pieces of cake. Last winter part of an eighteenth-century graveyard was torn away, scattering leg bones and arm bones and pieces of rib and hip among the smooth stones of the beach, and people went scavenging for skulls and didn't know what to do when they found one; perfect and so thoroughly human in spite of age and anonymity. For the first weeks after the storm the cliff looked freshly wounded with the strata of its history suddenly exposed: a layer of white shells, a wavy line of dark earth, orange sand, yellow sand, the movement of pebbles, and high up along the edge of the land you could see the dark little pockets of the graves that had been partially torn away; looking like the nesting sites of some unknown animal. If it were at all possible I would like to slice through my own thoughts like that; to say: look, there is the Emperor Napoleon pottering around in his newly-made garden, a grubby white dressing-gown wrapped around his heavy body and a red Madras handkerchief tied around his head, up before the dawn to water the passionflowers and the rose bushes. And there, in a lower deposit of time, is the Portuguese nobleman Fernando Lopez, with his scarred and broken face, working tirelessly among vegetables, flowers and fruit trees, and hemmed in from all sides by a wild green oasis. Within this same cross-section I can see a very old man I once met, standing in the forest of high oaks and chestnuts he had planted when he was still young. He is saying to no one in particular, 'It is quite amazing how fast trees grow.' I also find myself confronted by my father in his little suburban garden, enclosed by a low fence over which the bobbing heads of the neighbours can be seen and with aeroplanes roaring across the sky once every five minutes, and he is standing on his scrap of a lawn, admiring the stone head of a lion propped up on the rockery as if it was a distant monument on a hill.

Around the middle of 1819, when Madame de Montholon was preparing her justification for leaving the island and her husband was hoping to leave with her, and so was Madame Bertrand, St Denis the manservant and Pierron the pastrycook; then some of the servants decided among themselves that they must do something to improve the appearance of this place that they had all grown to hate so thoroughly. They began by turning their attention to the little attic rooms where most of them slept. The network of corridors that connected these rooms was open to the black room beams and thick with spiders' webs that brushed against their faces as they walked through, and the partitions separating one room from the next were made of rough wooden slats, covered with torn and peeling paper. They obtained a length of plain cloth, glued bright blue paper to it and stretched it along the corridor, making it look like the backdrop of a false sky on a stage. They obtained rolls of plain paper to cover the cracks in the partitions and Chinese wallpaper decorated with wood-block patterns for their bedroom walls: a different pattern for each room. Somebody remembered that when they first arrived a large canvas floor cloth had been laid under the carpets in the entrance room, so they lifted that up and hoisted it into the attic, cutting it to fit the floor of each room to hide the bare boards. When everything was ready they invited Napoleon to walk up the steep ladder that led to their quarters, so that he could admire the improvements. He paused to examine the imperial costumes that were hanging in the wardrobe in Marchand's room, pulling them out one by one and leaving them scattered in a heap on the floor. He was impressed by the panoramic view of the mountains and the sea which could be seen from Noverraz's room, but angered by an engraving of the opening of Waterloo Bridge which hung on the wall, demanding that it be taken down at once.

During this same time Napoleon was sporadically busy with dictating an account of the history of military fortifications, and in order to clarify his thoughts he had models made of the various configurations of ramparts, earth walls and ditches behind which an army could protect itself, and still be able to attack the enemy. It would seem as if the idea of constructing a garden around Longwood came to him while he was staring at these tiny defensive models, and perhaps also the work done in the upstairs attic rooms made him realise how easy it was to change the appearance of things and to please or even deceive the eye.

Longwood was exposed and overlooked on all sides. To the north and west there was Deadwood camp in the distance with its moving anthill of red-coated figures and the sound of drums and bugle calls, shouts and gunshot carried on the wind. By the gate leading into the garden there was the constant activity of the sentries on duty at the guardhouse. To the east the land fell away towards the steep cliffs above the sea, and the south was hemmed in by a distant ridge of bare mountains. The area that was called the garden had been fortified along its outside perimeter with ditches and earth walls, and patches of rough turf had been dug up and lain across these barricades to try to stop the loose earth from being washed away by the rain. Around the house itself there were no sheltering walls, no flowerbeds or paths; just an expanse of coarse grass and the occasional thin-trunked gum tree.

Napoleon began with the patch of land that could be seen from his bedroom window and from the west-facing windows of the entrance room and drawing-room. Together with Montholon he drew up plans for making a symmetrical flower garden, done in the classical style he had always favoured. There would be a raised, oval-shaped bed in the centre, surrounded and intersected by little paths, with flowerbeds on either side of the paths in which rose bushes and strawberry plants could be grown. A coffee tree would be planted at the centre of the tableau and the bright carpet of a lawn would surround the varied tapestry of flowers. Pierron was sent at once to Jamestown to buy a selection of spades and pickaxes, wheelbarrows and rakes, and within a few days what became known as Marchand's Garden had begun to take shape.

Once the initial work for this garden had been completed and there was nothing to be done except wait for the plants to settle their roots, Napoleon turned his attention to the patch of land on the other side of his private apartments. Another raised bed was made and this was planted with trees that soon grew so thick that once they were established the sunlight hardly penetrated through their leaves: this was Aly's Garden. Eleven Chinese were employed to help with the heavy work, and two of them who were particularly skilled as carpenters were instructed in a mixture of English words and sign language to construct a wooden trellised avenue that would lead from a door in the dining-room out into the depths of the new garden. Napoleon planted the seeds of passionflowers along the line of this trellis and within three months it was festooned with a thick covering of dark leaves and corkscrew tendrils. On every sunny day there was a fresh display of the surreal faces of the passionflower, each one as big as a saucer: purple, white and red and said to resemble Christ's crown of thorns and the nails that fixed him to the cross.

But no amount of dense greenery could keep the Trade Winds at bay, and Napoleon decided that what he needed was a high turf wall that would defend him from the air blowing in from across the South Atlantic Ocean. Montholon approached Sir Hudson Lowe and the Governor was very willing to send over a supply of men, horses and wagons to help build a barricade of earth along the eastern side of the Longwood garden. They constructed a semi-circular turf wall, nine feet high and forty feet long, with a broad path running along its inside edge which it was supposed would eventually become an avenue of trees.

Now Napoleon wanted to have fish to remind him of the ancient carp that had stared and gulped in the ornamental lakes of palaces and castles he had known. He arranged for a half-moon-shaped basin to be excavated near to the protecting turf wall, and this was lined with stone and cement and painted with several layers of oil paint as a final safeguard to prevent it from leaking. As soon as the paint had dried a hundred little red fish, acquired from Jamestown, were tipped into their new home, but by the following morning much of the water from the pool had seeped back into the ground and most of the fish were floating on their sides, colourless and dead. The survivors were put into wooden tubs and someone was sent to Jamestown to find the one-eyed plumber Mr Gordon, and to persuade him to come and re-line the pool with lead.

Until the early part of 1819, the supply of water to Longwood had been very erratic, but now a reservoir had been built up in the mountains at Diana's Peak, and a little pipe carried water down directly to Longwood and Deadwood Plain, although when rain was scarce the reservoir was quickly emptied. Napoleon decided that he would make use of this flowing water; he would have a network of canals and overflowing pools; he would have a fountain. A little channel lined with cement was made to divert a trickle of water from the reservoir through the turf bank, along the length of the path and into the half-moon pond. A cistern twelve feet square was built at one end of Marchand's Garden, and the water was carried there and on to a third pool made out of the tin bath Napoleon had used when he was first at Longwood. The new cook Chantelier managed to turn a piece of pipe into a fountain, and once this had been connected Napoleon had the satisfaction of stepping into his gardens and giving the command: 'Let the fountains play!' The cook would turn on a tap in the kitchen and a thin line of water would make its cautious progress along the length of the cement channels, with Napoleon walking beside it as it travelled and laughing with delight when it reached its destination and was thrown up into a column of dancing spray.

The work continued unabated. A bridge was built across the flowing water and there were benches made of turf where a man could sit and admire his surroundings. But what the place lacked was trees, and most especially, an avenue of tall trees. Napoleon felt that oaks would be best suited for the purpose and he arranged for a number of good-sized trees to be dug up from the other side of the island and transported on wagons to Longwood, with as much earth as possible clinging to their roots. When the oaks arrived, thick with leaves, they were planted in an orderly line on either side of the path by the turf wall, and carefully watered morning and evening. Not one of them survived the upheaval, however, and so a double line of fully-grown peach trees was planted instead, and some of these were able to resettle themselves.

A single cedar tree had been growing near the house and when this was accidentally cut through the roots and killed Napoleon decided to have a wooden aviary built on the same spot, overlooking the little pool made out of the tin bath. The two Chinese carpenters were responsible for the work and they made a complicated container which I am now looking at in a rather dim photograph here on the table in front of me. The aviary is divided into three separate floors and it stands on four dragon's feet with four dragon's heads sprouting out of the roof, and a delicate tracery of Chinese flowers, birds and trees decorating the woodwork in between the lines of the bars. A strange bird is perched on top of the roof; he is supposed to be an eagle, but with his hunched back and loosely hanging wings he looks much more like a cormorant drying his feathers after a dive. The Chinese had probably never seen an eagle and when Napoleon was confronted by their approximation of the king of all birds, he found it ridiculous and had it removed, although now that the aviary is on display in a museum, the cormorant-eagle is back in position. Even before this ornate prison was completed a collection of canaries was bought in Jamestown and set in little cages while they waited for their home to be made ready. But then they all caught some disease and died within a few days of each other and so the aviary was only ever used by a chicken, a lame pheasant and a few pigeons who escaped when the door was left open.

At the point where the channel of water was brought through the high turf wall Napoleon had the idea of making a grotto, and so a rounded hollow was excavated and the Chinese carpenters made decorated screens to hold the earth in place, and an archway and doors of carved wood. A table and chairs were set up inside the grotto, and on a few occasions Napoleon sat there to take his breakfast surrounded by dancing dragons and wildly flying birds, but when the earth in the grotto became dry it began to crumble through the lacework of the screens and the place soon lost all the charm of the original idea and was allowed to disintegrate.

During the final year of his life Napoleon thought that he would like to have a view from the garden out over the expanse of the sea, and so the Chinese made him one more strange and exquisite monument, a tiny teahouse set on a pedestal above the line of the turf wall, made out of carved wood and glass and lined with a drapery of white muslin. Inside this fairytale tower there was just enough room for a table and a single stool, and on its roof a Chinese dragon with a long tail twisted and turned to face the direction of the oncoming wind.

St Denis and Marchand have both left written accounts

of the making of the gardens at Longwood, and the way that the work seemed to wake them all out of the stupor of some enchantment. Instead of lying in his room like a chrysalis waiting for a change of season, Napoleon would be up by five o'clock in the morning, impatient for the cannon shot that signalled the withdrawal of the sentries from around the house. Dressed in his white dressing-gown and with the red handkerchief tied around his head, he would rush outside to plant new seeds, to water the roses and the strawberries, to arrange for trees and bushes to be moved like items of furniture from one place to another until the correct symmetry had been achieved.

Every morning during this sudden flurry of activity, he walks around the house waking his servants and companions one by one, throwing lumps of earth at St Denis' attic window and singing,

> Wake up, wake up,
> You are in a strange bed.
> You will sleep so much better
> When you have come home.

Shouting for Marchand to come down, 'Mamzelle Marchand' – as he called this gentle-faced man – 'Mamzelle Marchand come down, the sun is shining' and then Noverraz, Pierron, the cook, the groom, the Chinese, Montholon, Bertrand, everyone, everyone must come and be set to work. None of the Frenchmen had ever done this kind of thing before and Napoleon's own hands were so soft that they blistered easily when he used a shovel, but for as long as he was enthusiastic he expected the entire household to join him in his enthusiasm. They stopped for breakfast at around eleven o'clock, and usually Napoleon would retire to his room to sleep or read or take a bath, and then if the weather was still fine he would reappear in the afternoon to walk around his garden, admiring it and making plans for its future.

Captain Nicholls now suddenly found that his duties were much easier. In his diary he records seeing Bonaparte in October 1819, 'walking in his Gardens this afternoon about 5 o'clock, he had a handkerchief tied around his head and was in his dressing-gown . . . he appeared very fat.' In November the Emperor was playing with Bertrand's children in the garden; in December he had a spade in his hand and was at work superintending the transplantation of some young oak trees. In January 1820 he was wearing a large straw hat, and strolling contentedly across the grass, unbothered by the fact that it was raining. In that same month he was seen out in the garden at 5 a.m., watering his flowers even before the sentries had left their posts, and later in the day he was sitting and staring at the red fish in their tubs of water. In February he was impatiently awaiting the delivery of fifty peach trees that would form a new line of concealment right along the western boundary of his garden and in March, at six in the evening, he stripped off all his clothes and plunged into the cistern pool, while Count Montholon and two servants waited to help him out and dry him with towels.

It is from Nicholls' diary and from the diary of Captain Lutyens, the Orderly Officer who took over his job in February 1820, that the story of the chickens, the goats, the pig and the ox is best told, although St Denis and March- and also mention the same sequence of events. In spite of all the ditches and ramps, the walls and fences, it was still easy for domestic animals to make their way into the Longwood garden if they were determined to or if someone happened to leave the gate open. In the early weeks of 1820 Napoleon discovered a group of five or six chickens busily scratching up the pansies and the eternelles growing in his flowerbeds. He told St Denis to fetch one of the guns which he had not used since the days when he had gone out riding with Gourgaud; he took aim and managed to kill three chickens with one shot. A fourth chicken flew up on to a low wall with a clatter of noise, and that was shot as well. Napoleon ordered the spoils of his hunt to be taken to the kitchen, and said that no matter who owned them he would never pay compensation: the crime deserved the punishment. A few days later a goat belonging to Madame Bertrand suddenly wandered out in front of Napoleon while he was busy supervising the building of a sod wall, and that was shot, and in February another goat was discovered walking through the gardens at half-past six in the morning and Napoleon shot at it twice through the green painted railings of a fence. He told St Denis about the goats of Corsica which used to destroy all the sapling trees growing on the mountains and how he had wanted to destroy them all but his old uncle forbade him, saying that he was a fool, the goats were more valuable than the trees. Three more goats came trespassing later in the month and Napoleon killed two of them and when he missed the third he turned his rage against an empty wine bottle, shattering the glass with gunshot.

One day a young pig came hurtling through the garden and after a brief hunt it was killed and eaten for supper that evening. The last creature in this curious catalogue of slaughter was an ox belonging to the East India Company which was used for ploughing the land on a nearby farm. The ox, followed by several companions, blundered its way through a gate that had been left open and together they trampled with their heavy frightened bodies towards the inner sanctum of Napoleon's garden. He ordered two guns to be brought to him immediately, shot the ox through the neck, killing it outright, and wounded one of the others before the intruders were chased back into the surrounding landscape. Madame Bertrand's youngest son Arthur saw the animal toppling to the ground and he ran screaming to Napoleon and hid his face between the

Emperor's legs. The Orderly Officer and several soldiers felt it was their duty to warn Napoleon that he might have inadvertently killed one of the sentries. When Sir Hudson Lowe was told about the incident he was convinced that Napoleon had arranged for the ox to be driven into his garden so that he could have the pleasure of executing it, and he wrote an anxious letter to the authorities in England asking what legal action he should take if his prisoner happened to kill a man. Could he be tried in a court of law on the island and if he was found guilty of murder could he be punished accordingly?

Nevertheless Lowe was very pleased with the fact that Napoleon had discovered the pleasures of gardening. He wrote a letter to Lord Bathurst in London, describing the Emperor's new hobby, and received an enthusiastic reply saying that 'if there are any plants, either in the Cape or at any British settlement or in this country, which General Bonaparte may wish to add to his present collection, no effort on my part shall be wanting to procure and forward them to St Helena'.

During the same months that the gardens of Longwood were being established, the building of Longwood New House had finally got under way. Lowe had decided that the best and safest place to position this fine Grecian mansion was at a distance of some four hundred yards from Longwood Old House, as it was now to be called. This meant that while some groups of soldiers and labourers were busy helping Napoleon to create his garden, others were occupied with the task of constructing his official residence. By January 1820 the foundations for the new house had finally been laid: the outline of a building cut into the bare earth in an area where there were no trees, no flowers, no shelter from wind or rain.

CHAPTER XIV

The state of man doth change and
   vary,
Now sound, now sick, now blithe,
   now sorry,
Now dancing merry, now like to die;
Timor mortis conturbat me.

   William Dunbar, *Lament for the Makers*

I am sitting in what is called the Quiet Room, on board the RMS *St Helena Island*. We have passed the Bay of Biscay and that point called Finisterre which is always mentioned on weather reports, and we are making our way towards the Canary Islands. From where I am sitting I can look out of a wide porthole through which a triangular expanse of sea rises and falls with the movement of the ship. The room judders softly, the closed door rattles, and a table lamp designed to look like a ship's propellor rocks on its wooden stand. A clock on the wall ticks through the seconds, chlick, chlick, chlick, and when we pass over a large wave it makes another noise as it slides to one side on its hook. On that same wall there is a coloured lithograph which shows Brunel's iron screw steamship the *Great Britain*, tearing through the fierce waves of the British Channel in

1843. A line of small empty armchairs faces me like earnest visitors waiting silently for the moment when they are called, and behind them the porthole is flanked by two long chintz curtains on which peacocks perch in oriental ornamental trees and two butterflies, a white and a red, dance together on a cream-coloured background.

There are only forty passengers on board and most of them are Saint Helenians going home after a holiday in England or going for a holiday on the island to meet up with friends and relations. Some have not been back to the island for twenty years or more and there is a growing sense of nervousness in their anticipation. They all know each other or at least each other's families, and during these few days I have listened to conversations filled with the names of aunts and cousins, brothers and sisters; who is newly married and who is newly dead. I have spoken to four people who live in the area called Longwood, 'You know, where Napoleon stayed', and that already gives a different closeness to this story I am in the middle of telling. Yesterday I spoke to a small lean man whose name is Evidence. He is descended from someone who came on the boat that brought the Emperor to the island; hence the name, although I cannot understand what it is evidence of.

Before coming on the boat I was trying so hard to hurry Napoleon towards his grave that I forgot to mention the five men who arrived at Longwood in September 1819. They were Dr Antommarchi, the two priests Abbé Buono-vita and Abbé Vignali, the cook Charpentier who managed to get the fountain working in the garden, and another servant. This little band from Europe had been selected by Napoleon's mother, his brother-in-law and his sister Pauline, to come and join him in his captivity and to help him spiritually and physically for as long as he remained on the island. They were all, in their different ways, utterly unsuited to the task: one was old and suffering from the effects of a recent stroke; one was ill and about to become more so; two were almost illiterate country people and the fifth had no training for the job he was expected to do. It would seem that Napoleon's mother and his brother-in-law Cardinal Fesch had been persuaded by a clairvoyant that the Emperor had already escaped from St Helena, carried away from the island in the arms of angels or by some other providential means, and set down in safety and contentment in a distant land. So the five men had been chosen and sent as a token gesture, a way of pacifying General Bertrand from whom the urgent request for help had come.

The two priests and the doctor were Corsicans. Abbé Buonovita was in his mid-sixties, but many years of working in tropical countries had made him look much older and since his stroke his capacity for speech and movement had been seriously impaired. Napoleon tried to keep his distance from him, as if such a blatant example of physical frailty might be contagious. 'He seems to have come to St Helena only to get himself buried here,' he said, and asked the doctor to look after him as well as he could. The other priest was very different. Abbé Vignali was a poor shepherd who had become a priest in his own village area and this was the first time he had ever left Corsica. He was in his early twenties, small, dark-skinned and barely literate. 'A Corsican mountaineer with a savage and brutish appearance' was how one English doctor described him, and he shocked everyone with his habits and manners, although no one paused to describe the particularities of his behaviour. When Napoleon died it was Vignali who kept watch over the corpse, and I suppose that at some moment during his long vigil it was he who managed to remove the Emperor's penis and testicles so that he could keep them as holy and sacred relics. Vignali later gave the testicles away and they eventually found their way to that museum in southern France, but he kept the mummified penis and it was only sold after his own death. It was first acquired by an American publisher and book collector; then in 1968 it appeared at the Christie's auction of the Vignali Collection of Napoleonica, and again in a Paris auction room in 1977 when it was sold to a private buyer for the reputed sum of 7,000 francs.

Then there was the doctor, Francesco Antommarchi. He was thirty years old and up until then his training had evolved from his work as assistant prosector, helping the famous anatomist Dr Mascagni with the task of dissecting corpses. I once met someone who was involved in this same profession; he asked me if I would like to see the work he was doing and pulled a white cloth away from an object that stood on his table to reveal the head and shoulders of a dead man, the skin grey from the embalming fluid it had been soaked in and one half of the skull cut open to reveal some particular detail of the brain. I have been haunted by the beauty of that grey face ever since and by the extraordinary immensity of the cavity of the skull, but someone who has learnt to unravel the intricate mechanism of a dead body has no training in keeping a living body alive. When Napoleon questioned Antommarchi about his previous work experience he realised very quickly that this doctor with his silk socks and his abrupt smile would be interested in his patient only once he had ceased to breathe and he could examine him at leisure with a scalpel and a hacksaw. Antommarchi had the disconcerting habit of laughing with a sort of wild glee whenever there was serious talk about pain, mortality or religion. After one such outburst Napoleon said to him, 'I can forgive your foolishness and your lack of skill, but a want of reverence I cannot forgive,' and it was only when he was at the very end of his life that he allowed Antommarchi to treat him.

The new arrivals had a number of boxes with them. There were two crates of books, but these were mostly second-hand volumes that the priests had brought for their own amusement. Antommarchi had a bottle of rose water which Napoleon was quick to appropriate, and he also had Professor Mascagni's *Introduction to General Anatomy*, a large book filled with vividly coloured illustrations which Napoleon studied closely, especially the page which showed the liver and the internal organs situated in that same region. From his sister Pauline he received some fine toilet articles: a silver-backed mirror, a silver-backed hair-brush, sharp scissors, an ivory comb. From his mother he received some books and newspapers, a miniature portrait of herself and a little oil painting of his son the King of Rome, wide-eyed and angelic in white satin and looking older than he had ever seen him before. His friend Lady Holland had sent him some flower seeds for his new garden, and games and albums. I wonder what these games were; in one museum showcase in France they have a collection of Chinese wooden puzzles with the solutions drawn out on thin paper in a little book, and on the page lying open you can see a spidery and incoherent pencil sketch that was said to have been done by Napoleon himself, perhaps while he was trying to find a solution to a puzzle. But it must have been the Chinese carpenters who made these, and I have not seen anything else in the way of games except for the two chess sets and a pack of large playing cards, some of which Marchand used on their blank sides when he was writing out a draft of his master's will.

The priests had brought with them all the equipment necessary for the celebration of the Catholic Mass. They had exquisite vestments of white and gold, a chalice and a paten for holding the body and the blood of Christ, a font for the holy water, a vessel for the holy wine; all made of silver and lined with gold. They had two silver crucifixes mounted on crosses of black ebony, scented candles, lamps for burning incense. Napoleon liked the idea of attending a Mass, and suggested that they could convert the dining-room into a chapel. And so they set about transforming the appearance of that dark and windowless room that had often seemed like a cubicle for the damned in hell when it was lit every evening by a blaze of candles shimmering on silver and fine porcelain. They found a mahogany sideboard that was no longer used now that the ritual of formal meals had been abandoned and no guests came to be entertained, and they stood it on two low steps and called it the altar. They draped the sides of the altar with red satin hangings, fixed to the ceiling with golden hooks. They had white satin fringed with gold lace as an altar cloth, decorated in one corner with the letter *N* under a floating crown. To complete the effect Montholon cut the tassels and the gold trimmings from one of his dress jackets, and these were sewn on the altar cloth. From the same costume he removed four embroidered *N*s which were attached to the green velvet carpet covering the steps. Pierron the pastrycook transformed a corner cupboard into an intricate miniature palace of silver and gold and this served as a tabernacle for the host. Bertrand found a portrait of Christ which could be hung behind the altar, and the crucifixes were set on either side, along with the branched candlesticks, the incense burners and Chinese vases filled with flowers from the garden.

On the following Sunday everything was ready for the first Mass. The door, through which a patch of daylight could enter, was closed, the candles and lamps were lit, the air was made dizzy with the spiced smell of incense and at twelve noon the Emperor was courteously invited to attend the ceremony.

In his priestly costume, the Abbé Buonovita was able to transcend his decrepitude; the Emperor again looked more like an emperor, while his servants and companions, dressed according to their rank and gathered together in the flickering darkness, looked like the members of a royal court. From now on Mass was celebrated every Sunday, and when Napoleon was too tired or ill to attend, his bedroom door was left open so that the perfumed smells and the subdued chanting could reach him.

At this same time, with the garden growing up all around the outside of the house, the servants decided that they must do something to improve Napoleon's living quarters, and he agreed to sleep in a large brass bed in the drawing-room while they set to work. They covered the damp walls with a fresh layer of white paper, put striped wallpaper up in the bedroom and lined the study with swathes of fine calico cloth. They bought new curtains and carpets in Jamestown, mended and polished the furniture, stripped the little campbeds of their faded hangings and bought a fresh supply of bright green taffetta silk to enclose them. A couple of years previously Napoleon had arranged for a number of silver plates to be broken up and sold for the value of the metal, but he had kept the silver eagles that stood guard on the lids of the dishes, and these eagles were now made to perch on the posts of his two beds. I am not at all sure where they were fixed; looking at a black-and-white photograph that I have here I cannot see them, and when I was confronted by the originals in that glassed-off room in the museum in Paris I cannot remember noticing the imperious heads of eagles peering out from among the folds of green silk. Nevertheless Napoleon declared himself very pleased with the changes that had been brought about. 'This is no longer a bedroom,' he announced. 'You have made it into a whore's boudoir!'

So the days pottered along and between October 1819 and April 1820 the main events that took place must have been the shooting of trespassing farm animals. When the Orderly Officer Captain Lutyens saw Napoleon plunging naked into one of his own ornamental pools, this was probably because the plumbing in his bathroom had finally collapsed and some workers were busy for several days trying to do something about it, up to their knees in the black mud that had accumulated like silt under the bathroom floor. The floors themselves and the wood panelling on the walls had almost disintegrated and other rooms in the house were nearly as bad, with the damp erupting through the wallpaper and the swirling patterns of fungus and mould overwhelming the original designs. Because Longwood New House was going to be ready quite soon, it was felt by the Governor that it was unnecessary to bother about repairing the Old House.

Napoleon did walk over to inspect New House one Sunday afternoon. He admired the size of the rooms and the elegance of the furniture and said, yes, it was far better proportioned than the home he had got used to, but he had no intention of moving. The building had been partly dug into a bank of earth which protected it from some of the wind, but it was surrounded by a bare stretch of land without any trees or bushes and Napoleon said that he was not prepared to begin again with the work of planting and building. St Denis complained that although the rooms were indeed spacious, he found the furniture shabby, and there was nothing on the walls, no clocks or vases, no pictures; hardly any mirrors, so that the place had a neglected, unfinished appearance. All around the outside walls little covered niches had been made for statues, but since there were no statues to be put in them this only increased the impression that whoever owned the place had fled from it, leaving the shell behind. Perhaps the Chinese carpenters and the pastrycook could have combined their skills and constructed a line of statesmen, kings and philosophers, with Chinese features and real costumes billowing in the wind and the rain, but since the entire garden area was surrounded by the close-meshed metal fence that had been sent over from England they were never asked to, Napoleon insisting that he would never agree to occupy the building as long as this cage was in place.

In April 1820 Napoleon presented the Orderly Officer with a gift of some vegetables grown in his garden: green beans and white beans. Lowe was informed about this gift and it upset him a great deal because if the white beans were meant to represent the Napoleonic line and the green ones were the French Bourbon kings, then what message was his prisoner trying to communicate? He wrote an anxious letter to his superiors in London asking them what they thought he should do next, but he never received a reply. In May Napoleon was seen mounting a horse and setting off at a slow walking pace towards Deadwood Plain, stopping every few moments to survey the landscape with his glass. Lowe was informed, and guards were alerted across the island because it seemed as if at last the Emperor was planning to escape. Two months later Napoleon persuaded Vignali to dress himself in a white jacket with a red Madras handkerchief tied around his neck and, masquerading as the Emperor, to ride slowly towards Deadwood, stopping and staring and riding on. Lowe wrote another letter to London saying that the prisoner was becoming increasingly devious.

Whenever someone pauses to describe Napoleon at this time they say that he looks terrible: fat and shabbily dressed in a white dressing-gown that needed washing, his face grey and puffy as if he was suffering from the effects of the damp and the wind in just the same way as the structure of his house was suffering. Quite often he hid himself in a darkened room because he felt ill – he said that a knife was turning inside his belly and around his liver – but still he would emerge into the daylight and go for short walks around the garden or for a ride in his carriage. On a few occasions he even tried a ride on horseback, but this exhausted him utterly. In October 1820 he decided to go on what seemed like a major expedition, out to an area called Sandy Bay on the southern side of the island, where, so I have been told, you have a sense of being cut off, not only from the world, but even from the rest of the island.

Plans were made for a grand picnic, and on the morning of 4 October 1820, Napoleon and a group of his companions and servants, set off in a long cavalcade towards their destination. They were on their way to Mount Pleasant, an elegant house belonging to Sir William Doveton, who like the Balcombes five years previously, now watched the slow approach of these unexpected guests, and joined them with his family for a picnic on the lawn. Napoleon was jubilant although he looked dreadful, he drank three glasses of champagne and ate much more food than was usual for him. But then when it was time to leave he could scarcely walk, and his heavy body had to be supported on both sides as he staggered back to where the horses were waiting. He got home and went to bed, staying there for several days, deaf and giddy and dazzled by any bright light, with the shutters drawn, the blinds down and the room stuffy and hot, and in retrospect, this illness can be seen as marking an end to another aspect of his freedom.

CHAPTER XV

'What matters it how far we go?' his
    scaly friend replied.
'There is another shore, you know,
    upon the other side.
The further off from England the
    nearer is to France –
Then turn not pale, beloved snail, but
    come and join the dance.'

Lewis Carroll,
Alice's Adventures in Wonderland

Our first sight of the Canary Islands was of Tenerife by night; moving closer and closer to a glistening triangle of orange lights and behind them a high wavy line of mountains. In the morning we walked along a broad street past huge and glassy offices and hotels and blank areas of rubble and concrete where old buildings had been removed to make way for new ones. An avenue of trees led to a monument dedicated to a miraculous apparition of the Virgin that had taken place long ago, but I could not understand the entire text. A number of evergreen oaks in the avenue had died and they stood there with their trunks silvery grey and their branches lopped off like limbs and each one had a little notice hung around what you could call its neck, asking you to protect it from destruction but not saying how this should be done. We walked down a narrow sloping street to what must be the red-light district where short fat ladies in short tight dresses waited patiently outside the doorways of little single-storeyed houses. On the roof of one of these houses a band of scrawny cats lay about in the sunshine behind a shining barricade of broken glass bottles that had been cemented along the top of the wall.

We were in Tenerife for only five hours and then we were off again, watching that high island slip away until you could no longer distinguish the big pale buildings that clung to the land, but only the shape of steepness tipping down towards the water and up and up into the mountain ranges and the peak of the volcano that had first created this island; El Teide it is called, looking like one of those Hokusai prints of Mount Fuji, so symmetrical and serene.

On the morning of the next day the flying fish came, bursting out of the water like flocks of startled sparrows, wings outstretched and little fishy bodies hanging down so that their tails are buffeted by the waves and they skim and skid, further, a bit further, and then fall back into their own world. We entered the Doldrum Fracture Zone, where the sea was not rough but was pockmarked with deep indentations as if it was being pulled at from underneath, and the wind seemed to be blowing from all four directions at once. During that night there was a storm, a little one for the South Atlantic but big for someone who doesn't have any experience of storms at sea. You wake up out of a restless dream to a tremendous hubbub of noise and movement and your body is so busy with its own private battle that you can't ask anything of it. There is only passivity, the passivity of waiting for something to change, and you lie there throughout a long day, watching the reflection the waves outside throw on the ceiling of the cabin: a fleeting pattern of light and thin shadows that rushes with a relentless flickering energy like the shadow of smoke in a wind. If you don't want to look at that you can close your eyes, your body lurching with the ship and the noise of engine and air-conditioning and other unidentified hums and rattles all seeming to come from within the cavity of your own brain. And in that noisy darkness the thoughts race by in just the same way as the reflection of the waves race by, and you find yourself walking up familiar hillsides and into familiar rooms and seeing faces that you haven't seen for such a long time while in the background there is a relentless babble of words which is not quite a conversation and not quite a thought process.

In that strange daze of rough weather in a little cabin it was easy to imagine Napoleon as he lay in his darkened bedroom with rain and wind hammering on the shutters and the air inside dense and hot. Mosquitoes, footsteps on the attic floor above his head and along the corridors separated from him by thin walls; the sound of Mass being celebrated, the cannon shot at dawn, dusk and midday; the shouts of soldiers, doors opening and closing. Once in a dream he cried out and thrashed like a fish caught in a net, so that Marchand who was keeping watch over him that night went to wake him, shaking him awake. In his dream he had been about to embrace his wife and child, opening his arms and stepping towards them but losing them just at the moment when he touched them, and now he was angry at being woken because this tenuous thread had been snapped and could not be reconnected.

Between October 1820 when Napoleon drank champagne and ate potted meats with the Dovetons on the lawn of their garden overlooking Sandy Bay, and May 1821 when he died in the drawing-room at Longwood, nothing much happened. But even if he lay silent in a dark room he was still the Emperor, and every movement he made or word he spoke was recorded by the people who were with him, watching hour by hour. Sometimes his health improved sufficiently for him to be persuaded to go out into the garden and walk with slow steps leaning on someone's shoulder, or he might even go for a short ride in his carriage, keeping the horses at walking pace, but after such an expedition he would return to the house exhausted and the days and nights would again merge into a continuous block of time. Then the people who were with him hovered around the bed and murmured, uncertain as to what to do next, waiting for an improvement or a deterioration; filling letters and notebooks with accounts of the repetition of their duties and the drifting confusion of their daily lives while the Orderly Officer would be driven to peering through the slats of shuttered windows and begging for scraps of information that could be used to make up his daily report. Reading these accounts, by Antommarchi, Bertrand, Marchand and the others who could claim to have seen or heard something, makes me think of one of those nature films that document the life of a reclusive and nervous wild animal, following it into an underground burrow to watch it eat, scratch, fight, copulate, give birth in the darkness, and following it on brief forays into the outside world where it darts and hides for fear of being seen by an enemy. At certain dramatic moments such films change the speed of time, elongating it so that a flurry of fur, teeth and dry dust becomes an event which takes place with infinite languor and carefully choreographed precision. And always in the background you are aware of the odd fact that this intense excerpt from the life of one little creature has been made by filming it for hours, days, months, and then cutting out the most impressive pieces and connecting them together into one continuous sequence.

On 10 October 1820 Napoleon faints as he climbs out of the steaming water in his lead-lined bath tub, and he has to be carried to his bed. He stays there sick, cold and complaining until 16 October when Captain Lutyens reports catching sight of him walking unsteadily in the garden. On 8 November Sir Hudson Lowe, who is busy supervising the final work on Longwood New House, sees the prisoner taking a short ride in his carriage, with Count Montholon sitting next to him.

> As soon as they perceived me, the drivers were desired to turn off by another road, but this could not be done so soon as to prevent my having a good view of General Bonaparte's side face at about thirty yards' distance. He wore a round hat and green surtout buttoned over his breast. He appeared much paler than when I had last seen him. (Lowe Papers, 20,131)

For most of the weeks that follow Napoleon stays in his room, drifting in and out of a hazy sleep, and when he is seen to emerge for a ride or a walk he often has to be carried back to the house. Lowe is kept informed about each such expedition, but he remains convinced that any apparent frailty is all 'a damned trick'.

> It was all done on purpose to show off. Nothing but a trick so that his pale face might be seen. All a pretence to make people believe he is ill . . . Depend upon it he took an emetic in order to make him sick when in the carriage, that he might thus be seen by the English grooms, vomiting. (Kemble/Gorrequer, p. 187)

On 26 December Napoleon receives a bundle of old European newspapers and from them he learns that one of his sisters has died in August of that year. He sits in a chair motionless and speechless like a man in a trance, and during the following days be becomes even more remote from his surroundings and the people who are with him. However, by the middle of January he seems to be showing signs of improvement and Captain Lutyens reports seeing him in the garden sitting and staring at the water in the half-moon pool, walking with slow steps to the Chinese tea-house from where he could look out at the horizon of the sea, sitting near to the complicated birdcage that is now empty of all occupants. His face is 'as white as a sheet of paper. He seems weak and staggers when he walks. His body is bent. He is as fat as ever. He goes muffled up in a greatcoat and wears long pantaloons.' (Aubry, p. 473)

These months are the hottest of the year on St Helena and in order to avoid the sun as well as the wind, Napoleon has the idea of having a seesaw erected in the drawing-room, so that he can exercise his body without needing to leave the house. An enormous machine is constructed with a central wooden pivot four feet high, padded iron seats shaped like saddles and T-shaped iron handles to grasp on to. It is bolted into the floor in the centre of the room with the furniture standing around like a silent audience, and one of the seats is weighted with lead to counteract the heaviness of the Emperor's body. Count Montholon is the most frequent partner chosen for this activity, perching himself obediently at one end, facing his master, bouncing up and down, up and down. Sometimes Bertrand's four young children are also asked to participate: 'He had my sister, or two of my brothers, or me, at the other end of the seesaw, and thought it a great joke to give us such violent jerks that sometimes we were thrown off.' (Aubry, p. 477) But the machine was only in use for a fortnight and then it was taken apart and the floor was 'restored to its former condition'.

February 1821, and there is still March, April and the first days of May to go before the end.

The process of slipping away was slow and inexorable, and while reading about it you cannot avoid entering that claustrophobic house and standing there watching what is happening in the darkened room. He says that the machine has broken down, the lamp has run out of oil, there is no more blood in his body, the Devil has eaten the muscles of his legs, a knife is turning and twisting in his side. He lies there on his military campbed in the darkness and coughs, complains that his eyes hurt, drinks a little thin soup and one day is over. He sits in an armchair with a dim light coming from two candles burning in the room next door and someone is waving a cloth in front of his face to keep away the gnats and mosquitoes and another day has been and gone. He says that his feet are cold, his legs are cold, his hands are cold, and since hot water in a tub does not seem to help his servants swaddle his feet in steaming hot towels and at night they try to keep some warmth in him by enveloping his legs in a sack made out of thick flannel. He says that he is dizzy and deaf and lifting his eyelids exhausts him and he is afraid of the sound of the wind and distressed by any sudden noise which he hears in the house. If he wakes he asks to be left alone and if he finds himself alone he cries out for someone to come to him.

During the month of March Napoleon seems to drift away entirely, his mind preoccupied with private imaginings and associations, and since he is beyond the reach of those who are with him they turn their attention to the workings of his body, making a note of the food that it accepts or rejects, the medicines that are administered and what effect they have; the rate of the pulse, the colour of the skin, how many times he urinates and how often his sheets are changed. They roll him over, they rub him down, they spoonfeed him and brush him and comb him, encouraging him as a mother would an awkward child, and to alleviate his pain they offer him enemas and purgings, blistering and bleeding, calomel and arsenic, opium, ether and eau-de-Cologne. It has been said that Montholon, or was it Antommarchi, was paid by the French to poison the Emperor and it has been suggested that one of the English doctors might have taken on the same task on behalf of Sir Hudson Lowe. There is even a school of thought that believes Napoleon poisoned himself accidentally by ingesting the arsenic contained in the wallpaper next to his bed, turning his face to the wall and licking it like a calf hungry for salt. Maybe it is possible that the final process was speeded up by the doctors and their medicines but it seems unlikely that this was an intentional act, besides, there was no need to kill him since he was dying already, and as one of the English doctors said, the only cure for his sickness, whatever that sickness might prove to be, was freedom from the island.

Then on 12 April Napoleon surfaced from the dim, subterranean world he had been inhabiting and began to make his last will and testament. Marchand took down the details of the general outline of this document on the first day and on the following day Montholon was asked to write down a dictation of the first draft of the entire text. It was a detailed valediction of one man's entire life in which everything that belonged to him – money, objects of sentimental or financial value, shoes and medals, cups and watches, even the hair on his head and the heart within his body – was to be allocated to this or to that person with whom he had once been associated. There were bequests of money, much more than he in fact possessed, for all the many people whom he felt had helped him at various stages during his career, and if they were already dead, then it was to go to their wives or their children. There were money and gifts for most but not all of the companions and servants who had been with him on St Helena: a necklace of gold and diamonds for Marchand, a sum of two million francs for Montholon. A silver alarm clock was for his mother, lace for his wife Marie-Thérèse, a medal cabinet for one sister and a silver and gold candlestick for another. Every member of his family was to be given a ringlet made from his hair and his wife was to receive his heart in a sealed casket. To his son, in whom he saw his own direct link to immortality, he gave everything that was most personal to him: the cloak of Marengo, the silver washstand and the Sèvres plates, the medals and fine costumes, all the things that he had chosen to accompany him to St Helena and which he had first unpacked when he was a guest of the Balcombes staying in the Pavilion. Since he thought that he might be dying of the same disease that had killed his father, he asked the doctors to examine his internal organs very carefully and to provide his son with a detailed description of the state of the stomach. He was confident that Antommarchi could at least be trusted in his professional ability in this respect.

He would like to be buried in France, near to the river Seine, but if the British government objected and his body had to stay on the island then he chose to be interred at the Vale of Geranium, near the spring where he had stopped to drink in 1816 and from where he still got his drinking water, brought to the house in silver containers in a cart pulled by the Chinese. He dictated a letter that would announce to Sir Hudson Lowe that he had died 'as a result of a long and painful illness', and he discussed in some detail the arrangements that the household would need to make for returning to Europe once it was all over. The old priest Buonovita had already left the island, and he asked the young one, Vignali, to keep a vigil over his body until it was taken to be buried and to have a Mass said continuously throughout that time.

On 16 April he made a copy of his will from Montholon's dictation, sitting propped up in bed, the paper resting on a sheet of cardboard, and concentrating all his effort so that his handwriting was clear and legible. The work of adding further codicils continued on the following day, the Emperor dictating with his eyes bright with fever. Montholon said to Lutyens 'all his strength seems to have passed from his body to his brains. He is now thinking only of things of the past. His dullness is gone. His memory has returned and he talks continuously of what will happen on his death.' (Lowe Papers, 20,157)

The doctors were anxious that he move to a room with more air in it, and so he agreed to rest during the day in the drawing-room, although he still insisted on being returned to his bedroom at night, saying he felt more at home there. Carpenters were called in to repair some rotting floor-boards in the drawing-room and he lay in his bed and watched them at work.

When the will was completed and Napoleon was satisfied that he had done all that he could to secure his name and reputation after his death, his mind again started to drift. The English doctor Arnott, who attended him regularly during these last weeks, describes the Emperor sitting in his chair whistling, and then stopping abruptly and opening his mouth wide, projecting his jaw forward and staring steadily at the doctor with a vacant expression.

On 24 April he asks Arnott a long stream of questions, each one running into the next at a great speed. What do claret and sherry cost? Who screams the loudest on the battlefields, the English or the French? Is London more beautiful than Paris? Does the tide reach as far up as London? Is the water from the Thames good? (H. G. Bertrand, pp. 187–8)

On April 26 he interrogates Pierron the pastrycook about some oranges that had been brought up from Jamestown which he found bitter without sugar and even more bitter with sugar. Having completed his questions he begins again with the same sequence.

'Would these oranges become any sweeter if they were kept? Did the boat bring any limes? Any almonds? Any pomegranates? Grapes? Wine?

'On the whole, one could say it brought nothing. Did it bring any walnuts? Walnuts come, so I understand, from cold countries, and almonds from hot ones. Are the limes good here . . . ?

'Did the boat bring any limes, any pomegranates, any almonds?' (H. G. Bertrand, pp. 205–6)

Two days later he was again busy with Pierron, asking him if fruit syrups could be made out of cherries, out of apples, out of pears, out of almonds, out of walnuts. 'Which is more refreshing, milk of almonds or lemonade? Walnuts come from countries where the climate is colder and almonds grow in countries where the climate is warmer.' (H. G. Bertrand, p. 212) Do they make fruit syrups from cherries, apples, pears, almonds, walnuts?

On 30 April he calls Bertrand to him and asks him very formally, 'How is your family? What is the weather like? Is there any sun? What time is it?' He wants to know what has happened to the Russian aide-de-camp and the French one, and where is Gourgaud and why did he leave. Where is Dr O'Meara? 'Is he here or did they send him away because he was too fond of us? . . . And Mr Balcombe where is he? What, has he left? When was that? And his wife as well? Oh, how very odd. She really has gone.' And the final words are repeated ten times over as the thought strikes him again and again. (H. G. Bertrand, p. 222)

One night towards the end of April, Montholon, who is in the room with him, is woken up to hear Napoleon saying, 'Oh, oh Death,' and then, seeing his companion staring at him, he announces, 'I am dead my friend.'

He died on 5 May in the early evening, just at the time when the cannons were fired to announce the arrival of darkness. The bed on which he was lying was moved out into the centre of the room so that people could walk around on either side of him when they came to pay their last respects.

CHAPTER XVI

'You know,' he added very gravely,
'it's one of the most serious things that
can possibly happen to one in a battle
– to get one's head cut off.'

Lewis Carroll, *Through the Looking Glass*

I have been to St Helena and I have come back and now I am sitting at my desk looking out at a familiar bank of grass which has been burnt dry and pale during a long hot summer with no rain. The sky is blue with white clouds moving across it and the wind is pulling noisily at the thin branches of the tree outside my window.

When we first got home I set out everything we had brought from the island on the table in the room next door: the spoils of a journey. The collection looked very naked and forlorn taken out of context like that. There were several stones including three big honeycombed lumps of basalt that had been rubbed smooth by the sea; a group of bottles, some of them seeming to be very old; thick-lipped shells; fragments of broken pottery picked up because they bore the image of a Chinese fish, the corner of a castle, flowers, the head of a unicorn. There was a piece of twisted wood that might be ebony since it came from the area where the ebony once grew; the skull of a cat from among the prickly-pear cactuses at Lemon Valley and the skull of a dog from a rubbish tip at Deadwood Plain; a postcard of Longwood, tinted in overlapping blocks of bright colour: pink for the house, green for the grass, blue for the sky.

All over the island you can find a stiff thick-stemmed plant which they call Old Father Never Die, and I now have three pieces of that growing in pots. From the vicinity of Napoleon's empty grave I have a strange-looking cactus that makes tiny reproductions of itself on the tips of its blotched finger-like leaves, and from the garden around Longwood I have a little bunch of the dry and thistly yellow flowers which the French call *éternelles*; a strange choice of a name since they maintain the appearance of life when they are in fact dead and lifeless.

Before we left the island our next-door neighbours gave us a tray with Napoleon's head and shoulders cut out in silhouette from a piece of ebony and inlaid into the soft, almost pink-coloured wood of a St Helena pine. We also have a couple of glass bead necklaces made by an old woman who lives out at Blue Hill, and a couple of seed necklaces, one of which began to swell and germinate after it had accidentally got wet. Then there are photographs, mostly landscapes, and a quantity of notes, both hand-written and typed, in which I tried to keep a record of the immediacy of certain meetings and certain places, and to which I now turn in order to continue with the narrative of this journey.

Ascension Island was nothing like I had expected it. I had been sure that its outlines would be sharp, even jagged, and its colour an almost uniform grey, and yet in the distance I could see the soft rounded shape of hills: one dark red, one pale red and another almost black. Coming closer the hills seemed to be made of a fine dust blown into symmetrical heaps and there was nothing growing on them: no trees, no grass, not even a rough scrub. Roads were drawn into the sides of these hills as if a finger had traced a line in the dust, and dotted all over the landscape there were bulbous white shapes like mushrooms at various stages of their development, and some of these held supplies of gas or petroleum while others were used in communicating with a satellite system.

We never went ashore because the captain did not want any further delays, and so for a couple of hours we lay at anchor quite far out in the bay while extra passengers were brought to the ship in a motor launch, and a car and a number of large boxes were heaved out of the ship's hold with a crane, lowered on to decrepit-looking barges and towed away towards the shore. If you threw something overboard: bread, chocolate, an apple core, even a piece of wood, then the surface of the water immediately became thick with the jostling black bodies of trigger fish. The cook caught two of them and cut the tail off one to use it as bait to catch more, and it lay there on a green oil drum, its colour fading as it gulped in the bright sunlight.

The final two days of the journey were hectic and noisy with so many extra passengers on board. Men, women and children were sleeping on the floor of the Quiet Room and under the awnings on the deck and sometimes two stereo systems played loud music at the same time and nobody noticed. For several hours we watched as the silhouette of St Helena grew larger and more defined and the closer we got the colder the weather became with clouds hanging over the steep outline of the island and a thin rain falling steadily. We were taken ashore in a little motor launch just as it was getting dark, the sea black and clear and the cliffs on either side of Jamestown rippled and folded like huge curtains pulled across the water. We stepped out one at a time on to the stone landing stairs, with a dangling rope to grab hold of and a man there to grasp your arm and steady you if the waves suddenly lurched you forwards. Then we walked along the narrow quay and into a shifting and shuffling crowd of people who were waiting behind the customs sheds, silent and expectant.

So here I come full circle, walking through a crowd of strangers beside a high wall, over a bridge, through a stone archway and into a town where everything is familiar because I know so much about it and yet utterly strange because it is like waking up to find yourself surrounded by the landscape of a recurrent dream. We climb into an old taxi that smells of oil and leather and sink into deep seats in which you sit like a child staring up at the world around you. We drive past the botanical gardens where the people stood with torches in their hands waiting to catch a glimpse of a man called Napoleon and past the house that has been built on the site of the house where he stayed that first night, pacing up and down in a small room with the uneasy knowledge that he was on the edge of a different stage in his life. Then up a steep hill leading out of town, but going towards Plantation House, not towards Longwood. The road is narrow and edged by a stone wall on one side and the cliff face on the other and in the darkness we can see the lights of the ship in the bay and the lights of the streets of Jamestown. And this must be as good a place as any to turn to the thought of Napoleon recently dead, lying on his bed in the drawing-room at Longwood on the evening of 5 May 1821.

During that last day it was decided to open the shutters, the curtains and the windows that had been kept closed for so long, breaking the candlelit spell of darkness in which everyone in the house had been moving and making it possible to watch with accuracy what was happening: to see the sweat on the face, the slight heaving of the chest, and to know exactly at what moment it was all over. Then Madame Bertrand stopped the clock at eleven minutes to six, Dr Arnott went out of the room to send a message to the Governor, Dr Antommarchi closed the lids of the eyes, and Bertrand, followed by Montholon and the other members of the household in the order of their rank, stepped up beside the bed to kneel and kiss the hand of the Emperor. A man was sent to Jamestown to try to obtain some plaster with which a mould of Napoleon's face, head and hand could be made; workmen were instructed to hang the ceilings and the walls with black cloth and a chandelier was brought in, filling the room with its flickering light.

Sir Hudson Lowe had been informed early in the morning that his prisoner was expected to die on this day and so, together with a group of doctors and officials, he made his way to Longwood New House, sitting in the newly painted rooms among the elegant English furniture, waiting for further news. At six o'clock when he was told that Napoleon was dead he hurried to the front door of Longwood, standing once again on the little wooden-framed verandah, demanding to be let in. He was told that he must wait until the chamber and the body had been made presentable, but two of his doctors were allowed to go in so that they could add their signatures to a death certificate.

During the next few days before Napoleon's body was finally lowered into a stone-lined hole in the ground, there was a great deal of activity all over the island. All the soldiers at the military camps and on the ships in the bay knew that they would soon have to leave, and the islanders knew that they would soon have to adjust to a sudden drop in the population. The value of goods and property fell overnight and, as one soldier wrote home to tell his mother, a horse that had been worth £70 on the previous day would now be lucky if it fetched more than £10. St Helena was turned into a vast ant heap with figures scurrying this way and that, carrying messages and packages, trunks and packing cases, wood and stone, pick-axes and rolls of black cloth. Longwood was at the centre of it all, the inner sanctum in which the dead king was lying, helpless but still demanding attention. In the uncertainty of what should be done to him and where it would be best to do it, his attendants were to be seen lifting up his heavy inert body and carrying it from one room to another, from bed to table and back to bed; washing it, shaving it, dressing and undressing it, drawing it and casting it in plaster, and taking from it a number of intimate souvenirs by which the Emperor could be remembered, later, when this was all over.

A report was drawn up to certify that Napoleon was dead. The letter which he had written for the Governor, announcing his own death, was sealed and delivered and the packages containing his will and the codicils were opened and read. Vignali withdrew into the dining-room to pray for the recently departed soul, and since they were no longer needed, the sentries who guarded the house were dismissed, making the night much quieter than it had ever been during the six previous years. For a few hours Napoleon was left to lie on his bed undisturbed, with Marchand, St Denis, St Denis' English wife and the English doctor, Arnott, sitting in the room with him, but then at midnight Montholon and Bertrand were called from their beds to come and supervise the proceedings while the Emperor was washed and brushed, shaved and perfumed with his favourite eau-de-Cologne and wrapped up in a white shroud with only his head showing. St Denis said that his own hands shook as he helped with this work and it was as if the cold body was charged with a 'sort of electric property', but everyone agreed that the Emperor looked beautiful when they had finished with him. He appeared like a man in the prime of his life, younger than his years, smiling slightly with a private contentment, a tinge of colour to his cheeks and his skin of a translucent marble whiteness. It was probably during the night that Dr Arnott embarked on the first attempt to make a death mask of the face, pressing the features into softened candlewax, but he was not successful. They moved Napoleon on to the other campbed which they placed between the two windows with a little table on either side at the head end.

At six in the morning according to Bertrand, but about an hour later according to everyone else, Sir Hudson Lowe presented himself at Longwood, with fifteen companions including five doctors. The French were ready to meet them, dressed for the occasion, bowing, beckoning and standing stiffly to attention in the drawing-room, just as they had previously done when the Governor had come to visit their Emperor. Lowe stood before the bed and stared at Napoleon. He asked the man standing next to him to confirm that the deceased was indeed the person he believed him to be, and then he clicked his heels, saluted and left the room, with most of his companions filing out after him.

It was agreed that the autopsy would be performed at two o'clock that afternoon, and before then several people were given permission to make a likeness of Napoleon. An English captain, Frederick Marryatt, produced a curiously stiff little sketch in which Napoleon, wrapped in his shroud, appears like a large white grub, with a human head and a soft, shapeless body. A government official, Denzil Ibbetson, did a misty portrait in oils which gives Napoleon a long, pale and strangely reptilian neck and a jaw which seems to be hinged somewhere at the back of his skull. I wonder if Bertrand made his pencil sketch at this time as well; it is a nervous scattering of thin lines which just manage to indicate that a group of people are standing around a body lying on a bed, but although nothing is clearly defined in that picture it does possess an intensity which all the others lack. It was Bertrand who noticed how Napoleon's face on that first morning looked ten years younger than he really was, and then as the hours of the day moved forward his face seemed to race through the years so that by the afternoon he was beginning to look like an old man. (H. G. Bertrand, p. 234)

They decided to perform the autopsy in the billiard room; a trestle table was erected and covered with a white cloth and the body was brought in and placed upon it. A total of seventeen people had come to witness or take part in this strange ceremony, standing clustered around the table and watching as Napoleon was opened and examined piece by piece. Eight doctors were present but it was Antommarchi who did the work, dressed in an apron and at last able to demonstrate his expert skill with the scalpel and the hacksaw. Assistant surgeon Rutledge agreed to help with the business of detaching the organs; Vignali was to take notes on the proceedings for the French and Dr Henry was ready with paper and pencil to provide an account for Sir Hudson Lowe.

On the occasions when Napoleon had allowed Antommarchi to examine him he always complained bitterly about the coldness of his hands – 'Don't touch me, warm your hands first' – but since he knew that this man whom he disliked so much was at least expert in his own subject he would question him closely about anatomy. Cutting the nails of his fingers he pauses, staring at his hands, 'Tell me, doctor, what are the nails, the beard, the skin, made of? How are they formed, what is their function?' 'What is the function of the intestine, what is the shape and the appearance of the liver?' 'Doctor, you have known the human body so intimately, have you never found the soul when you were at work with your scalpel? In which organ do you think it might reside?' (Antommarchi, vol. 1. pp. 161, 201, 218)

Dr Henry notes that the head of the deceased is large in proportion to the body and the face has an expression of intense tranquillity. The skin is white and delicate, the hands and the feet are small, the hair is fine and silky, the shoulders are straight, the hips are broad. The sexual organs are extremely small, something which he thinks might help to explain the absence of sexual desire which the deceased had shown throughout the time of his captivity. When Antommarchi has opened the cavity of the chest he takes note of the fact that the kidneys and the heart are loaded with fat, and the heart is smaller than might have been expected. The inside of the stomach is in a very unhealthy state, but the liver about which Napoleon has so often complained appears to be quite normal, if a little on the large side. Sir Hudson Lowe's second-in-command, Sir Thomas Reade, was especially anxious to see the liver because there had been so much talk of the climate of the island causing hepatitis and other fatal diseases, and so Antommarchi held it, red in his hands, and slit it open with one deft movement saying, 'See, it's perfectly good, perfectly sound, there is nothing extraordinary about it.' (Lowe Papers, 20,214)

Antommarchi was very interested in Napoleon's head. He took exact measurements of the skull so that he could interpret the character of the deceased 'according to the craniological system of Drs Gall and Spurzheim', and from this he could deduce that the organs of conquest, ambition, deceit, kindness and imagination were prominent. He was eager to proceed further with his researches and to remove the brain itself, 'that object of the highest interest', from its casing of bone, but those who were present in the room stopped him, or as he put it, 'My proceedings were unfeelingly arrested,' and so he was not able to discover more about Napoleon's ability and personality.

The heart and the stomach were set on one side, and since there was nothing sensible to keep them in, the heart was placed in a silver sponge box that was part of Napoleon's toilet case, while the stomach was placed in a silver pepper box, and both receptacles were filled with alcohol. Before sewing up the body Antommarchi must have seized a moment when the English were not watching him to extract two little fragments of bone from the rib, one of which he gave to Vignali, the other to Coursot the butler. Presumably this was also the occasion when he removed an ulcerated piece from the lining of the stomach which he later gave to Dr O'Meara and which was kept at the Royal College of Surgeons in London until it was destroyed by enemy bombing during the Second World War. Watching all this from the distance of so many years it does seem as if some ancient and obscure ceremony was being performed, with everyone who was present wanting to take for themselves a portion of the power of a dead man.

When the autopsy was completed the body was bathed for a second time. The hair was shaved from the head so that it could be made into bracelets for Napoleon's family and taken as mementos by the many people who were eager to possess a small lock of it. Almost everyone present cut out a piece from the bloodstained sheet on which the body had been lying, although according to St Denis the English took by far the largest share.

They dressed him up in the uniform of the Imperial Guard, 'green turned up with red breeches, and long boots, a good many Orders on his breast, sword by his side and cocked hat on, spurs, also on', (Darroch in Lutyens, p. 191) and carried him through to the bedroom where he had said that he always felt more at home. One of the campbeds had been made ready for him, covered with the dark blue cloak of Marengo and with white curtains twisted up the four bed posts. The walls, the floor and the ceiling were draped in black and the room was lit with candelabra and torches with a chandelier hung from the ceiling. Bertrand, Madame Bertrand and their children, dressed in black, positioned themselves at the head of the bed, and Vignali knelt at the altar which had been brought in from the chapel. The diamond star which Betsy Balcombe had seen glinting in the sunlight when Napoleon was making his way towards her family home, was again fixed to his breast.

The Emperor was now ready to receive visitors. On that first day, 6 May, nearly all the officers and private gentlemen on the island assembled outside the house waiting for the moment when they would be allowed to enter. Around six o'clock they were admitted in groups of four, six or ten persons at a time; through the billiard-room, the drawing-room, the chapel that had been the dining-room, into the bedroom and after a few minutes out again through the glass door that led to Napoleon's covered walkway in the garden. One soldier described what it was like 'suddenly coming out of the glare of the tropical sun and into the partially darkened room . . . Gradually as the contents of the apartment tumbled into shape the person of Napoleon . . . grew out of the comparative gloom.' (E. L. Jackson, p. 238) A young Scottish soldier writing home to his mother described the stillness of that room in which the only person who seemed to have life was the attendant who stood at the head of the bed and kept the flies away from the face.

Napoleon was on display throughout the following day, and it was then that the bulk of the inhabitants of the island, masters and slaves, men, women and children, came to wait in the garden of Longwood, and when their turn came, walked through the rooms of the house, and stopped to stare at the man who had been at the centre of St Helena for the last six years, staring at him now just as they had on the evening when he first came ashore.

CHAPTER XVII

A great while ago the world begun,
With hey, ho, the wind and the rain.

Shakespeare, Twelfth Night

I have been trying to re-enter the landscape in the area around Longwood; to see myself sitting there in the bleakness of Deadwood Plain and sheltering from the wind with my back to a clump of flax, its leaves rattling like cardboard swords. I asked a boy who was driving some black cattle through a gate if the wind ever stopped blowing and he laughed uneasily with his face turned away from me and said no, it never stopped. In the distance I could see the dark and vast silhouette of the mountain called the Barn, and near to me the ground was littered with all sorts of objects: the desiccated carcass of a prickly-pear bush, the cylinder of a washing machine, a car engine and other things that could no longer be put to any use.

When we were walking near the place where Napoleon's

house stands in its well-kept garden behind a stone wall and a thick belt of trees, I heard a sound that seemed to be someone shouting the rhythm of a song and there on the other side of the road was a young woman, as mad as the wind, roaring to herself and walking this way and that, examining the ground for something she seemed to have lost. We went into the shop where they sell beer and soft drinks, tea, chocolate and petrol, pig food and chicken food, watched by a group of young men and women who sat on the road, leaning against parked cars and drinking from cans of beer. One of them was mad too, with a fine-featured, elegant face; his head lolled to one side and his expression shifted and slid from despair to laughter to fear with no point of focus anywhere.

On the first occasion when we went to have a look at Longwood, the museum was closed for lunch and so we set off towards Deadwood Plain in the direction of Horse Point and Hold Fast Tom, with the Barn always ahead of us in the distance. We drove past concrete houses painted in bright colours, past a slaughterhouse, a home for backward children, a golf course, and stopped the car with the track going on in front of us, down through an expanse of open country that tipped towards the sea cliffs at a gentle incline and was cut across by little river valleys. This was the land that had been known as Great Wood, where ebony and gum trees and other trees that were never named and have left no traces to be remembered by, were once crowded together in all directions as far as the eye could see. It looked as if a war had been fought here at some point in the past and the armies had moved on, leaving the land scarred by all the activity that had taken place. Whatever soil there once had been was now washed and blown away to reveal the volcanic marl, which is like a sort of clay, pink, yellow, beige and grey, and where the wind or the rain had got a hold on it, its surface had been eaten into so that its sides had split open and great chunks of the stuff had crumbled and broken off.

To the west we could see a flat expanse of thin grass where the soldiers who guarded Napoleon had set up their living quarters and where a few cows were now grazing disconsolately. The track that we were on followed an incline towards the sea, flanked on both sides by the island's rubbish tip, with heaps of black plastic bags smelling of whatever they had inside of them and ungainly bits of metal lying around like the wounded on a field of battle. There were also large grey mounds of a powdery consistency that had apparently been dumped here by the lorry load and some of these had odd things protruding out of them as if they had taken root: the springs of a bed, a pig's jaw bone, the skull of a dog that I took home with me. The only vegetation was the odd clump of flax or prickly pears and a fat-leaved plant that crept close to the ground and produced the most extraordinary bright flowers: luminous pink, salmon pink, lemon yellow. The Barn was the backdrop to the entire area, seeming to watch over it. The new French Consul at Longwood said that wild albino cats and dogs lived there; in which case they must come like ghosts at night to raid the rubbish tips since there cannot be much in the way of food among those crumbling rocks. I think he also said that a St Helenian family lived in a house somewhere at the back of the Barn, but I might have misunderstood his carefully enunciated but difficult English.

Before coming here I had read about how the Barn bears an unmistakable resemblance to the profile of Napoleon, and I had imagined him staring out beyond the military camp at this vast and immobile reflection of himself. Now that I was there I could see what I thought must be his face: the hat tipping down into the sea, the nose and chin sharply defined against a pale sky and the body lying chrysalis-like, as it did when it was wrapped in its shroud. I took a photograph of it, with washing machines and succulent plants in the foreground and the line of the mountains set against the sky, and although the face is not quite as obvious now as it seemed to be then, I can still recognise the features quite clearly. However, since coming home I have reread those descriptions and I realise that my Emperor is the wrong way round; while I have him on his back with his feet pointing inland, they have him gazing out at the horizon, his hat merging with the bulk of the mountain and his neck climbing up out of the Atlantic.

There is a bronze cast of Napoleon's death mask at Longwood. It is set upon a white column and it stands in a cordoned-off area between the two white-curtained windows in the drawing-room where his bed was positioned when he died. The face looks very calm, exceedingly calm, but somehow blank and expressionless. When I was a child we used to have a photograph of William Blake's death mask on a wall somewhere in the house and he had such a look of intense, almost angry concentration about him that I felt uneasy when I walked too close to him, as if the eyes would suddenly stare at me or the mouth open to speak. I suppose Napoleon must have lost his concentration as well as his remarkably youthful appearance during the forty hours that elapsed between the moment of his death and the time when a successful copy of his face was finally made.

The head at Longwood rests on an ornate bronze pillow with pleated edges that curl up around the back of the skull and over the ears. The three other heads that I have seen in other collections are all without this pillow, but looking at them it becomes apparent that the ears are either absent or very oddly crumpled and there is no back to the skull. This is because the making of Napoleon's death mask was such a difficult business; the right materials were not available and no one on the island had ever done such work before and on top of that so many people wanted to be involved in producing it that once a fragile plaster likeness had been made then they fought over it, stole it, and invented elaborate stories to prove a particular right of ownership.

On the night of 5 May Dr Arnott had tried but failed to capture the transient beauty of the face by pressing it into a lump of softened candle wax. On 6 May Dr Antommarchi obtained some rough plaster that had been found near Longwood, but it was much too porous and a proper mould could not be made from it. During that night the attendants guarding the corpse tried to do something with a piece of silk paper soaked in whitewash, from which they managed to produce a vague approximation of Napoleon's features. However, it was the Englishman Dr Burton who was the most skilled and successful in the enterprise. According to his own account he was told that gypsum crystals, from which a sort of plaster of Paris could be made, were to be found at a place called George Island, and so on the night of 6 May he made a dangerous journey in a longboat to this little island which lies some distance from Shark's Valley on the eastern coast, and there by torchlight he collected some crystals, brought them back, roasted them and crushed them and turned them into a fine white powder. There is however an alternative version to this story which appears in the private diary of Lowe's secretary. He makes no mention of the sea journey by night but says that Burton went around Jamestown buying up plaster figurines, and having spent twenty pounds and ten shillings on the busts of kings and emperors, the bodies of goddesses and anything else he could find, he pounded them all together until they were of a unified consistency. Whatever the truth might be, Burton arrived at Longwood on the morning of 7 May and with the help of the groom Archambault and the Corsican doctor Antommarchi, he produced one mould of Napoleon's face and another of his ears and the back of his skull. He was only just in time since by now the body was beginning to decompose and the stench that permeated the room was almost unbearable. A young English soldier who was watching some of the proceedings wrote a letter to his mother in which he said that he could not get the image of the face out of his mind or the smell of death from his nostrils and his hands. When the task was accomplished Dr Burton placed the two halves of Napoleon's head on the mantelpiece in the drawing-room and left them there to dry while he returned to his quarters at Deadwood Plain.

On that same day the preparations for the funeral began. Napoleon had said that if he must remain on the island then he would like to be buried in the Vale of Geranium, close to where two large willow trees were growing, and the owner of this piece of land, a tradesman called Mr Torbett, was persuaded to accept the sum of £650 for 'damage caused to his property' and a further £50 a year to cover any futher inconvenience for as long as the body of the dead Emperor should remain there. Soldiers were ordered to start digging a pit twelve feet deep, eight feet long and five feet wide, and others were set to work constructing a track that would lead down from the road to the site.

Napoleon was to be buried in four coffins made to fit closely into each other like Russian dolls, and three of these were delivered to Longwood on the evening of 7 May. The first was made of tin with a mattresss and a pillow of white satin, the sides also covered with white satin, and the body, fully clothed, with long riding boots and a hat on the head, was lowered on to this gleaming bed. Unfortunately the coffin was a little too narrow and a little too short and so the hat had to be removed and placed across the thighs; even then the heels of the boots were pressed tightly against the silk. Madame Bertrand begged to be allowed to take the heart in its silver sponge box with a silver eagle on the lid, but her entreaties were to no avail and the container was soldered shut with an English shilling and placed next to the body. The pepper box with the stomach was placed alongside it, although Antommarchi very much wanted to keep it, saying that it would serve as proof that no medicines could have saved the Emperor. A number of objects were tucked around Napoleon and under his legs: a silver sauceboat made to look like an antique lamp, a plate; knives, forks and spoons engraved with the imperial arms; several gold and silver coins embossed with the imperial head; a silver flask containing water from the Vale of Geranium; a cloak, a sword and a loaf of bread. However it quickly became apparent that there was not enough room for all these things, and so, according to one account, the sauceboat, the flask of water, the sword, the cloak and the loaf of bread were all removed. George Rutledge, the English assistant surgeon who had attended the autopsy and guarded the corpse during the last couple of nights, decided to add a small metal plate to the other items, on which he had scratched his own name, 'as being the last British officer who had ever seen the deceased'. It was this same Rutledge who was involved with the silk paper and the whitewash and who later claimed that he saved the Emperor's heart when it was about to be carried off by a large rat. Just before the coffin was closed Bertrand took Napoleon's left hand in his own and clapsed it briefly. The lid was then soldered and the tin coffin was lowered into the mahogany one and screwed down and into the lead one and soldered again. Bertrand noted in his diary, 'It is said that with the air excluded, the body will be preservd for centuries.'

On the following morning Napoleon was encapsulated in the fourth coffin which was made out of a dining-room table belonging to one of the island's residents. The enormous and heavy succession of boxes was then balanced on wooden trestles that had been set up within the metal frame of one of the military camp beds, and draped in a cloth of purple velvet and the cloak of

Marengo. Any visitors who still wanted to come and pay their last respects were allowed to enter the chamber and sprinkle the coffin with holy water. It was at some time during that same day, 8 May, that Dr Burton arrived to make a cast from his moulds, and when he had finished his work he left the image of the front and the back of Napoleon's head to dry on the mantelpiece. While they were there someone managed to make a rough second copy, either from the broken mould or from the cast itself, and Madame Bertrand decided that although she had failed to obtain the heart she could at least appropriate the front part of her Emperor's face, and so she took it and packed it away in one of the trunks that was being got ready for the voyage to Europe. So when Dr Burton arrived for the funeral on the morning of 9 May he found that all that remained on the mantelpiece was the 'back or craniological part of the skull'. According to one account he was so angry he threw this piece to the ground and smashed it; according to another he took it with him to England, but it got mislaid after his death a few years later. The new French Consul said that quite recently they had found fragments of the mould somewhere near Longwood and he now had a perfect cast of Napoleon's ears in his writing desk upstairs. No, we could not see them, and there was no point making a fuss trying to prove their authenticity since the experts always get so angry about this particular subject. No, he would not say where or how they had been found but he was convinced that the island was still filled with Napoleonic relics; not long ago they had discovered the altar stone from the Longwood chapel which a local farmer was using to grind his snail poison on. Even during the short time that we were there we had the sense that there were many places where you could dig or search and find strange treasures. We met someone who had just unearthed a headless alabaster Buddha from his rubbish dump, and someone else found two blackened but perfect eighteenth-century silver meat-dish covers, sitting unnoticed in a cupboard in a house. Then there was that old lady out at Blue Hill in a place so remote that it was like being on an island within the island and on her verandah she had a classical chaise longue, with chickens perched nonchalantly on its beautifully carved wooden frame; so why not the ears of an emperor, found in a cattle barn or behind a shed?

At 11 o'clock a requiem mass was said at Longwood and then twelve British grenadiers came into the bedroom to heave the coffin on to their shoulders and carry it through the drawing-room and the billiard-room and down the six steps that led from the verandah into the garden. There a hearse was waiting; it had been made out of Napoleon's own carriage from which the seats had been removed and a flat top substituted. Sir Hudson Lowe was standing in the sunshine on the lawn, along with a number of other important figures, all of them in the full costume of their rank, with their heads bare in honour of the dead. When the coffin was in place and had again been draped with its purple cloth and blue cloak, everyone took up their position, on horseback or on foot, and the funeral cortège began to make its slow progress towards the grave.

The Corsican priest Vignali led the procession. He had just quarrelled with Montholon about what he should wear for the occasion but finally agreed to put his gold embroidered robes over the simple white ones. Behind him came the hearse pulled by four of Napoleon's horses. Bertrand and Montholon walked one on each side at the front while Marchand and one of Bertrand's sons were at the back. St Denis followed and behind him came the groom Archambault, leading a horse that Napoleon had called Sheikh, although its previous name had been King George. Then came the rest of the household servants from Longwood, and behind them Madame Bertrand and her children in a carriage. Sir Hudson Lowe and his companions followed on horseback and once they were on the road that leads from the Longwood gates towards Hutt's Gate and the Devil's Punchbowl, all the soldiers who had been guarding the island lined up like a human hedge along the left side of the route. The regimental bands played a solemn funeral dirge that had been composed especially for the occasion and guns and cannons were fired in a repetitive, echoing salute. The soldiers joined the back of the procession as it passed them by, and the inhabitants of the island had come to crowd themselves across the steep face of the landscape so that they could also watch what was happening.

When they reached the track leading down to the Vale of Geranium, the troops came to a halt and positioned themselves along the road as if they were preparing for battle. The coffin was lifted from the hearse and carried to its final destination by teams of grenadiers. The hole dug in the ground had been lined with flagstones taken from the kitchen floor at Longwood New House, and there were other slabs of stone waiting to cover the coffin once it had been lowered into position. A strong beam attached to two wooden triangles had been fixed above the hole, and there was a pulley attached to one of the branches of the trees. Everything: the grass, the stones, the beam, the branch, was covered with swathes of black cloth.

CHAPTER XVIII

'I often think he must like the cemetery
he is in. It is near the zoo and you can
hear the lions roar.'

Nora Joyce, in Brenda Maddox, *Nora*

About a year ago I went to visit Napoleon's tomb at Les
Invalides in Paris. It was a bright clear autumn day and the
sun was pouring into the grand entrance of that grand
building in a dense block of yellow light. Soft triumphant
music was playing on loudspeakers and a notice on the
wall asked visitors to be silent and respectful at all times.
An Englishman and his wife were standing behind me in
the queue to buy tickets and when their turn came he
suddenly launched into a vigorous argument with the man
who sold the tickets, saying that it was all far too expensive, much more expensive than it should be, and anyway
his family had important Napoleonic connections and right
now his wife, standing here next to him, was wearing an
antique brooch in which a lock of the Emperor's hair was
sealed and would the ticket seller care to have a look at it.

The ticket seller was not willing to examine the brooch and after some more angry words the Englishman paid his money and began to show his wife around, inspecting statues and memorial plaques with a proprietorial air. Down in the subterranean part of the building where Napoleon's coffin stands like a huge shiny lump of moulded chocolate watched by a circle of Grecian caryatids and surrounded by his own words and deeds carved into slabs of white marble, I approached the man and asked if he might be so kind as to show me the brooch. It was a small and pretty thing with a convex glass panel behind which you could see a little bunch of thin brown hair, of about the right sort of colour and wispy texture to belong to the person it was supposed to belong to. It was I believe the Englishman's great, great, great uncle who had been on the island when Napoleon died, and had obtained this delicate trophy which he brought back home with him and set in a suitable container of gold and glass. Now whenever I think of Les Invalides the Englishman's strident voice overrides the sound of reverential background music and when I remember walking through that opulent monument for a dead emperor, the little brooch hangs suspended in one corner of the image like a speck of dust on a lens or a bundled-up fly in a spider's web.

The tomb on St Helena is very different to the one in Paris. It is a quiet and peaceful place with only occasional visitors coming to interrupt its solitude. Nevertheless, even though the coffin and its contents were taken away long ago, and the plain stone that once marked the grave has been removed and replaced with a substitute, it still seems to be filled with the presence of a dead and buried man. I recently read an article about a retired accountant who uses a metal coat-hanger as a dowsing rod with which he can locate the exact position of the walls, windows and doorways of churches that fell down long ago and are now covered by grass and earth and forgetfulness. Sometimes he might sketch out an area where stones and bricks should be lying but when the archaeologists come to dig they find nothing there. This can be simply because he has made a mistake, but often it has turned out that he was locating a part of a building that had lain there concealed and undisturbed but was then dug up and removed many years ago. This phenomenon, of finding the memory of something that has vanished and left no trace of itself, is called by dowsers 'remanence'. At Napoleon's empty tomb on St Helena you get the sense that even if all evidence of that place of burial had been removed and there was no signpost to point the way down the track, no metal fence around a slab of stones, and even the chamber in which Napoleon was lying had been dug up and shipped back to France, someone like that man with his metal coat-hanger would still be able to delineate the outline of a large coffin in a stone vault, buried deep under the ground.

To get to Napoleon's tomb from Jamestown you follow the same route that he took on the first morning of his arrival. An old stone bridge leads out of the town, crossing what was a stream although now only a trickle of water runs along a concrete gulley and the rest has been channelled into metal pipes. Near to this bridge there is an area where the island's whores used to live and work in a square of low houses known as the Cattle Yard. I met a woman who was on the island in the 1940s and she visited the Cattle Yard one day by mistake and found herself unexpectedly surrounded by a crowd of women leaning over their open stable doors waiting for trade. But all that has changed now. The houses and the women have gone and the one ship that comes regularly into the harbour brings only a few cautious foreigners with it.

The road goes up the hill, following quite a gentle incline on this side of the valley, and to the right there is a turning which leads to what remains of The Briars. The entire property was bought by the Eastern Telegraph Company some time in the late nineteenth century; the Balcombes' family house was neglected and allowed to fall into ruin, the avenue of trees was cut down and the garden ran wild until there was nothing left of it. However, the Pavilion where Napoleon had stayed for the first three months managed to survive and it was enlarged and turned into the Company director's private residence, perhaps because he liked the idea of sharing his house with the memory of an emperor. Then in the 1950s it was bought by a descendant of the Balcombe family and presented to the French nation and now it is a small and stiff little museum with polished wooden floors and pale blue walls, fine prints and empire furniture, but not much that gives a smell of its earlier history. When we were there some workmen were putting up a new ceiling in one of the original rooms and I asked them if there was anything left of the attic where Las Cases had been proud to live with his son, hearing Napoleon breathing through the night beneath him, but they said there was no attic and never had been as far as they knew. I asked the guide if an unnamed portrait of a lady was of Betsy Balcombe as she appeared in later life and he said it might but but he wasn't sure, the guide who knew such things had unfortunately died a few years ago. The Pavilion stands in an elegant garden with brick pathways and ornamental trees and all around it the Cable and Wireless Company has scattered the landscape with evidence of the nature of their work. Huge reels of black and yellow cables sit about on rough grass among sections of concrete pipes, pieces of metal equipment and bright yellow vans. On the morning of that particular day they had just completed the installation of a satellite dish that turns its blank white face to the sky waiting to receive messages from the rest of the world, and everyone was very excited to see whether it would work as it was meant to do.

Where the Balcombes' garden lawn must have been, the

marks of Napoleon's horse's hoofs briefly cut into the grass like new moons, there is now a rather fine social club built in the 1930s out of corrugated iron and wood and looking like something from a Hollywood western. On a notice board fixed to an outside wall there was a mysterious typed message that warned all visitors not to stroke a black-and-white guard dog that was to be found wandering loose in the Company's grounds. Apparently this dog was in the habit of rushing enthusiastically towards strangers and then biting them if they returned his greeting. The message went on to say that if anyone ignored this warning and got bitten by the dog they would immediately be deprived of their membership of the social club.

From The Briars you continue along the road, with the Heart-shaped Waterfall which Betsy found so beautiful in the distance, and through a landscape of rock and cactus and low trees that reminded me of a dim childhood memory of a holiday in Corsica. Red cardinal birds and yellow canaries dip and dart among the bright vegetation and mina birds scream angrily at each other. They had not yet arrived on the island when Napoleon was to be seen clattering over the goat paths in his high riding boots. You go past Button Up Corner, Captain Wright's Corner, and then comes Alarm Cottage which is the first house along the side of the Vale of Geranium, leading to the spring and the tomb and beyond that the house of Hutt's Gate where the Bertrands used to live and where now a very old and tiny lady runs a shop which has almost nothing to sell. It is easy to miss the white signpost on the left which looks like something from an illustration in a book of nursery rhymes, standing stiff but leaning slightly forward with *The Tomb* written in careful black letters and pointing to a grassy track among trees.

I walked down the track on my own. Although at the time of the funeral it had been a bare hillside, with only a grove of willows growing close to the spring, the way is now lined with Norfolk Island pines and cedars. The track which the soldiers made at such short notice is flanked by a wall of earth with bright mosses, maidenhair ferns, and clumps of arum lilies clinging to its steep side. It was quite a long way from the road to the tomb, long enough for you to have a growing sense of anticipation as you followed the track round a slight bend towards a clearing lit by dappled sunlight. There was a figure of a man standing there, watching me as I approached, but he was standing so still, partially covered by the spattering of light and shade, that I thought he might be a tree which seemed to look like a man. When I got closer he began to move about, busying himself with cutting at the carpet of plants on the ground and seeming not to have noticed me until I spoke to him. He had been working here for the last six years, raking, cutting, sweeping and watching the slow advance of the occasional visitor who walked solemnly down the track as I had just done, and then stood and stared and probably took a photograph before turning and walking back again. He said he got very bored with the job of keeping watch over an empty tomb and he wished that more people came; when the weather was bad and there was no ship in the harbour, he might well be on his own for weeks on end.

The last of the willows that stood near the spring disappeared a long time ago, and three fat-trunked Norfolk Island pines planted in the 1860s stand in a little clearing with a thick forest of trees behind them. White lilies and a creeping plant with red flowers cover the ground around the tomb, with its enclosure of metal railings and its plain stone face. It was odd to stand in such a green silent place and to imagine the reverberation of noise and activity that had taken place here when the track and the grave had only just been cut into the bare hillside.

As Napoleon's coffin was lowered on pulleys into the stone-lined hole in the ground, a shout of command released the first volleys of musket shot, and then cannons from the coastal forts and from ships at anchor in the bay answered with a regular booming salute until the valley where the ceremony was taking place thundered with noise, and the event must have seemed more like a battle than a burial.

Once the coffin was in position, a slab of stone was swung out over the grave and lowered until it rested on the stone sides of the vault. Hot cement was poured over the cracks to seal off this, Napoleon's fifth container. Then with Vignali saying the prayers for the burial of the dead, red earth was heaped into the cavity, and since the final flagstones from the kitchen floor at Longwood New House had not yet been brought, some planks of wood wrapped in black cloth were placed on top of the raw soil, looking, so one soldier said, like a black door leading into the ground.

The entire ceremony lasted between one and two hours and when it was over, with no speeches said and no inscription marking the name of the man who was lying there, people began to leave. The soldiers on the road above the track set off back to their barracks, playing pipe music as they marched. Some of the English and French who were standing around the grave broke off little branches from the willow trees to take with them, but when they had gone there was a sudden rush of activity as soldiers and islanders converged on the trees, stripping them of branches and twigs to keep as souvenirs or to set in water until the white roots began to sprout and a new tree could be planted.

Perhaps on account of this desecration, but also as a way of finalising the whole business, Lowe ordered that some of the metal railings from Longwood New House be brought to the site. These were the same iron railings that formed 'the perfect iron cage' Napoleon hated so much, saying he would never consider entering that building as long as they were in place and 'if they were there for the security of his person they disgust him and if for ornament it does not accord to his taste'. An enclosure like a metal playpen was erected around the tomb, a final hindrance to stop the occupant from escaping or to stop anyone from getting too close to him, and a second outer perimeter was fixed in place around the entire area.

As a further precaution a guard of three soldiers was ordered to keep watch over the tomb, day and night. Tents were put up on the site on that same afternoon and later a hut was built to provide more adequate shelter. One of the first of these guards was the same young soldier who had written to his mother saying how he had watched over the dead Napoleon and how the look on the face and the smell of the room had haunted him. He wrote again on 13 May while he was on duty at his post by the grave. The weather by then had changed and the warmth and sunlight of a few days before had been replaced by wind and rain with a gale sweeping through the Devil's Punchbowl and into the Vale of Geranium that was already known by its new name, The Valley of the Tomb. The soldier told his mother how the wind was rattling over the planks wrapped in black cloth which were still covering Napoleon's grave, and how 'I have a sentry promenading on each side of it, to catch him if he gets up.' On the previous day two Frenchmen had come to ask him for a sliver of wood from one of the willows and although it was against regulations and Sir Hudson Lowe had not granted them official permission to make this request, he relented and gave them a little branch which they divided into two pieces and stuck in their hats. He also allowed them to come close to the grave and drink some water from the spring.

I have seen numerous bits of those willow trees: some are like fragments of old bone, set in glass cases in the company of hair, blooded cloth, a piece of wood from the coffin, a piece of rib. Others have been cut into the shape of tiny ornamental trees, like the one that is described in an auction catalogue, that droops over 'a small TOMB, beautifully wrought in Pure Gold, about *one inch and a half* long and *an inch* wide. It contains a figure of Napoleon in fine Gold, about an inch long, and inside the cover of it under a glass shade there is some of the EMPEROR'S Hair. It stands on a small Plinth which was made out of a piece of the Rock that forms Napoleon's Grave. There is also, suspended over it, a small Branch of the identical Willow that grows over the Grave. (Catalogue of the Sainsbury Collection, 1840)

CHAPTER XIX

Are not the trees green,
The earth as green?
Does not the wind blow,
Fire leap and the rivers flow?
Away melancholy.

Stevie Smith, 'Away, Melancholy'

I was very nervous about going to Longwood. In my mind the house and the garden had become like a place I had known when I was a child but had not seen since. I could look at the avenue of peach trees, the pond made out of a bath, the Chinese dragon on top of the little tea-house turning its face towards the wind, and I needed only to concentrate my memory in order to see everything with a bright, almost disconcertingly bright, clarity of detail. But what I could not do was to step back a few paces in order to relate the different things to each other, to set the house within the garden and the garden within the wider land-scape that lay beyond it; to walk through the succession of rooms looking back at the one and forward into the next. And I knew as well that just as with childhood memories, I had distorted certain images: the bath in which Napoleon lay, his white body steaming in the hot water, had become an enormous container as wide and as deep as his tomb. The dining-room with its red walls was utterly dark and oppressive even on a bright sunny day, while the garden was a strangely confusing maze of earth banks and mounds, ditches and ponds, and the trellised walkway that led out from Napoleon's bedroom was so covered by a tangle of passionflowers that you could never see if a person was within it.

I had also in my mind introduced myself several times over to the French Consul who had been living there for thirty-five years, and whom I had seen once, young and bearded, in a photograph taken shortly after he took up his post on St Helena. I had practised asking him questions about the house and the ghosts that I had been told he sometimes heard quarrelling in the rooms around him, and whether the wind always blew and whether he could see the profile of the Emperor in the rocks of the Barn and what he thought of the island, the English, time past and time present.

On the first occasion that we set off to visit Longwood I misjudged the distances on the map. There was no jolt of recognition when the walls of the garden appeared directly in front of us and I thought we still needed to take a turning off to the right; so we went past the house and down a steep narrow road that petered out entirely once it had reached a bridge, a donkey and a corrugated-iron shed. When we had finally looped our way back to where we started from the museum was just closing and it was only possible to walk hurriedly around the elegant garden staring at the house with its shuttered windows and its walls painted a bright earth red; doves flew noisily above the roof, and gardeners were busy among the lawns and flowerbeds.

We came again two days later. The old Consul whom I had expected to meet was somewhere at the back of the house, busy writing books about Napoleon and Napoleon's family, and the new Consul came out to greet us. He conducted us slowly and courteously from room to room, explaining as he went about the colour of the walls, the construction of the floors, where the things that were here had come from and where the things that had been taken away were now to be found. He pointed out that not a scrap of the house was original apart from the stone steps leading up to the front entrance door. Everything else had either been eaten through its heart by the termites which moved around the island like locusts, or had been destroyed by neglect and the bad weather. This, the last of several reconstructions, had been started in the 1930s, and it could now be considered accurate in its proportions and in its overall appearance. But keeping such a place in good order was an enormous task; the exterior of the building had to be repainted every year because the wind and the rain made it like being on a ship out at sea, and the interior was always being threatened by damp and termites. The garden was also a problem; Napoleon had done things in order to achieve a quick and temporary effect and they had to reproduce his intentions in such a way that they would last for many years to come. Peach trees are easily transplanted and quick to take root, but they are also quick to die, and so they had been replaced by rows of cedars and oaks. The barricades and mounds of earth behind which Napoleon had sought to hide himself from the soldiers and the wind, began to crumble and fall even within the same year as their construction, and so they now had a stone wall around the limits of the garden and little paths bounded by stone borders and sunk a few inches deep marking the exact route that the old paths had taken. They had built the grotto, but without the heavy bank of earth on either side of it, and so it stood like a temple dedicated to a simple and undemanding god: a grass-covered mound, perfectly shaped, with a little glass-panelled door leading into a small dark room where a table and a chair had been placed: no channel of water, no Chinese screens to hold back the cascade of falling earth, no mud or confusion.

The birdcage with the Chinese eagle looking like a cormorant perched upon it has been moved to a museum in France where it takes pride of place. The half-moon pond was destroyed long ago, but an exact replica has been made out of concrete: small and ungainly in its shape with goldfish swimming under the lily leaves. The pond that was made out of Napoleon's tin bath is still there, at least I think it is the original and not a copy, and it is also filled with lilies and fish.

In one corner of the garden, by a stone wall that had once been an earth bank, there was the Chinese tea-house, painted blue and white with little concrete steps leading up to it and the inside hardly bigger than a telephone box. It had been impossible to find a weather-vane cut out in the shape of a dragon and so they had set up a more traditional cockerel instead; perhaps it had also been felt that a dragon would have given a less dignified impression.

Not far from the tea-house there was the trellised walkway, a tubular cage built out of wood and painted dark green, leading from a door in the house out into the garden, like those cages that direct lions and tigers out into the circus ring. Nothing was growing on it apart from a few dry and brittle tendrils of a passionflower that appeared to be very dead and a jasmine bush that was beginning to creep rather tentatively along one side, close to the ground. The new Consul was hopeful that the jasmine would eventually be persuaded to cover the entire structure; the problem everywhere was the wind and the weather. To prove his point he took me to a part of the garden where the wind blew at you as if it was being forced through a long cold tunnel, and a few stunted trees were bent this way and that, trying to avoid its force.

I stood on the original front steps of Longwood, listening

to the doves and waiting for the gardener to come with a key for the front door. I entered a room soaked in the muffled light of closed shutters and drawn curtains. The air smelt of cedar wood and wax polish. The Consul drew back the curtains and opened the shutters and there was Napoleon's original billiard table on which he never played, covered with a white cloth. The room was painted a bright eggshell blue, the wrong colour apparently but it was due to be painted a regency green within the next few months. Two globes, one of the world and one of the heavens, stood to attention by the door leading through to the drawing-room and I looked to see if it was true that the tiny dot of this island in the South Atlantic was ringed around by the marks of fingernails and fingers pressing on it, but it seemed quite smooth.

The drawing-room was decorated with a white paper with a blue block print; an exact copy, based on the only surviving fragment of wallpaper torn from the walls shortly after the house was left empty. There was the death mask standing on its column and set between the two windows, and above it a lithograph showing the deathbed scene with twenty people weeping around the bed of the dying man. I then went through to the dining-room which was dark and oppressive with its red and gold wallpaper and almost no daylight coming through the glass panel of a door. It seemed impossible that so many people had cramped themselves into this small space to go through the formality of eating and talking with the candlelight shining on the silver. The original sideboard table that was used as an altar was there; it had belonged to a local shopkeeper who had finally agreed to part with it.

The first of the two bedrooms was quiet and light with white muslin cloth on the walls and white curtains and the low campbed stripped of its covering like a skeleton. The next bedroom had the other campbed in it, but made up ready for sleeping. The whole house was much smaller than I had expected it to be but these rooms were tiny; tiny beds, tiny bedside tables with delicate spindly legs, a little chair, a little scrap of carpet, a little desk; it was as startling as seeing that white horse in a glass cabinet in a Paris museum, looking more like a dog than a horse.

The bathroom was a terrible place. The walls were painted a dark brown and the bath in its wooden box was set in a far corner at the furthest distance from a little window. The bath was a narrow, steep sided trough, so deep that only the top of a person's head would show above its edge and the metal was black with a green tinge to it. There was no allowance for comfort except for a little hand-hold set into one side which I suppose was to help Napoleon heave himself up to his feet; I wondered if this was the soap dish that I had expected to see worn by the rubbing of a hand. If the light in the bedroom was impressive then the darkness in the bathroom was even more so. There was something almost frightening about the idea of a fat naked man sitting in such a deep trough in such a dark room, reading books about politics and military strategy with the steam rising up around his face, and the floors and the wood panelling of the walls disintegrating in the dampness. I could not see how he could have remained in that bath for two or three hours or how he could have read his books while sitting there. I could not imagine why he would want to sit here at all except that the hot water eased his itching skin and in the heat and steam of that room he must have felt as if he no longer existed.

A new staircase has been built to the attics where Napoleon's servants had once rumbled around in such close proximity to each other, with the rain and the heat coming through the tarred felt of the roof and each small partitioned space stifling during the day-time. A little gate barred the way and there were buckets and cleaning things on the steps. I asked if I could look into the attic and the Consul had no objections but said it had not been made to look like the original. Indeed there were new roof beams and new slate tiles, all in perfect order.

I bought two postcards, one tinted and one plain, and thanked the Consul at the gate. He smiled a lot and said we must come back again in ten or twenty years and by then the garden would be as he wanted it. Just before we parted we had a brief disagreement about the number of people who were living on the island in Napoleon's time and for a few moments it was as if we were fighting for the ownership of an area in the past. What do you think you are doing, he seemed to say, walking around a house that is not yours? What do you know about the proportion of the rooms, the direction of the paths, where it is that we found the Emperor's ears that are now in a writing desk in a room that has not been shown to you, because it is private?

I never went back a third time to Longwood, but stayed on the other side of the island, out of the wind. The place had saddened me. Although I had known that the house must have gone through many changes and had often been close to complete ruin, it had never occurred to me that the structure of the thing did not exist any more, or that it could have risen out of its own ashes more perfect as a replica than it had ever been in its daily reality. I suppose I would have found it more appropriate to see it as it appeared in the years immediately after Napoleon's death when the French had all gone home and a machine for cutting up sugar beet was stabled between the two windows in the drawing-room and the wallpaper with its pretty Chinese woodblock prints was torn off in strips by people who wanted something to take away with them, to prove where they had been.

It must have been very odd for the French going back to Longwood in the early afternoon when the funeral ceremony was over. To see the place with different eyes now that Napoleon was no longer within it. To move from room to room, opening curtains, shifting objects and pieces of furniture, looking at things that were familiar but that had changed in the process of being separated from their owner.

On the morning of the following day, 10 May, Sir Hudson Lowe arrived with his secretary in order to have a look at the property of the deceased.

He carefully examined all the portraits, the Emperor's clothes, his toilet articles, the snuffbox for Lady Holland and the one for Dr Arnott. He expressed the wish that Lady Lowe might also see them. She had asked to see the Emperor's room just as it had been during his lifetime. The Governor was told that if Lady Lowe would like to come on the following Monday, Madame Bertrand would show her everything and that all the China would be displayed so that she could see the different pieces. (H. G. Bertrand, p. 241)

Because each one of the rooms in the house had lost its original purpose, with the furniture pushed into corners and Napoleon's possessions bundled into boxes or cupboards, Lowe suggested that it would be a good idea to get everything out and put it on display. This would give a number of people the opportunity of 'seeing anything curious or valuable amongst the effects which had been left', and would also make it easier for the French to prepare a detailed inventory which could be checked by the Governor before everything was finally packed away and removed from the house. Napoleon had left a number of small personal items in three wooden boxes which had been locked and sealed by him and three of his companions shortly before his death, and although Lowe did not insist that these were opened at once, he said that he would need to inspect them as well and only then could he go ahead with the necessary arrangements for the departure of the French.

And so the household set to work again. The black cloth which covered the walls and ceiling of the bedroom was stripped off and the walls of the two bedrooms and the dining-room were rehung with fresh white muslin drapery, giving them a 'neat and comfortable appearance'. The bedrooms in particular were in a state of 'extreme discomfort' but they were cleaned and rearranged until they appeared to be as they had been during Napoleon's lifetime. Everything was put back in its familiar position: the beds were made up with sheets and blankets, a footstool was placed by Napoleon's favourite armchair and the flannel bag in which he kept his legs warm was folded up and put beside it. The red Madras handkerchief, the flannel vest, and other articles of simple clothing were laid out over a chair, ready for the Emperor to get up and get dressed and go out to work in the garden. The chamber-pots were under the beds, the portraits were on the mantelpiece, along with the alarm clock that had once belonged to Frederick the Great and the silver flasks which held water from the spring in the Vale of Geranium. Toilet articles and old uniforms were on show in the sitting-room; many of the clothes looked very threadbare and faded, startled at being brought out into the daylight after so long spent in the darkness of trunks and cupboards. The billiard room was used to display the china, with fifty-three plates set out on two tables along with silver forks and spoons, silver dishes, sauceboats, lids.

On 11 May, between the hours of five and six, Lady Lowe, the Governor and all the members of staff from Plantation House, went through the rooms looking at everything. On 12 May the Governor came to open the three sealed boxes, examine their contents and close them again with his own seal. On that same afternoon the house was 'thrown open to every person of a respectable class, in regular turn, to see it'. Soldiers and officers from the military garrisons were let in first and the inhabitants of the island were allowed to enter between four and five o'clock.

Once again I return to that young soldier who wrote letters to his mother telling her about everything that was happening during these few days. He was given permission to leave his post at the grave to come and look at Napoleon's possessions, moving with the others through the house from room to room. He describes the museum that presents itself to him, 'his bedrooms arranged exactly as they used to be when he inhabited them', family portraits on the walls.

> His clothes were all laid out in one room. I tried on one of his cocked hats. He must have had an extraordinary wide head, for it would not fit me when put on square (the way he always wore it), but did when put on fore and aft . . . the eagle with the crown on his head and lightning in his grasp, was everywhere. There was a dessert and coffee service of china, the most beautiful, I suppose, that was ever made. On each plate was represented some action of Nap's; but, the most curious plate of all was one with the map of France on it.' (Darroch in Lutyens, p. 196)

The soldier says that he is shocked by what he calls the 'wretched state' that Longwood is in, and with the same untroubled directness that allows him to try on the dead Emperor's three-cornered hat, he tells his mother 'I could not have lived as he did, I am sure, half the time that he did'.

CHAPTER XX

So out went the candle and we were
left darkling.

Shakespeare, *King Lear*

Now with Napoleon under the ground, surrounded by
mahogany and tin, stone and earth, I find myself for the
first time since starting this story, pausing to wonder why I
have chosen to trail behind the final years of this particular
man's life. I have never, as far as I can tell, had any special
interest in Napoleon, except for perhaps a sideways curiosity in the idea of someone choosing to be at the centre of
such a hot steam of pomp and noise, costume and ceremony. On the one occasion that I went to Versailles, the
pink tautness of the skin of his face in those vast and
brightly-coloured portraits of him, made me uneasy,
almost embarrassed. I moved with the rest of the crowd
through rooms that are far too large and down staircases
that seem to have been made for giant opera singers, and
like a child who goes to the zoo and is delighted by the

pigeons that come to peck at some dried bread, I found my attention caught by some tiny fossilised shells that were embedded in the stone steps leading down a hallway. I wondered if these stones had been chosen especially, or if such delicate remnants of movement and life had not even been noticed when everyone was busy building Versailles.

I still know very little about Napoleon before he came to St Helena, but while writing the chapters that are so far completed, I have grown accustomed to his presence, so that it seems as if I have often encountered him sitting inert in a darkened room, or have seen him like some familiar, ancient, speechless relative, walking cautiously through his garden. Even after his death I have continued to watch him as he was dressed and undressed, opened up and closed again, and carried from one room to another. I saw his coffin lowered into the ground; hot cement poured over the cracks in the stones to make them airtight; geraniums, tuber-roses and violets planted in the fresh earth; and I saw guards and visitors illing around the grave, distracted, preoccupied with the knowledge that this stretch of time had come to an end and they would soon be leaving the island that had been holding them so tightly. And there I find myself, also distracted, trying to work out as one does when someone dies, in what way I have been connected with this person, and what I am left with now that he has been removed from sight. It is curious to realise how passive I have been; following in the footsteps of my thoughts without a clear idea of where they were leading me, and as an aspect of that process, going to St Helena just so that I could accumulate a few fleeting impressions.

For almost a month we lived in a little concrete bungalow on the western side of the island, not far from Plantation House. The taxi driver who collected us from the harbour took us to her home where she gave us an evening meal of fish cakes, porridge and cups of strong tea turned bright orange by the evaporated milk, and then she brought us to our destination, rattled the glass doors open, and found a switch that flooded the green walls of the sitting-room with electric light.

During that first evening I turned on the transistor radio and the only connection I could make was with Radio South Africa, which told me that I must immediately shake off the slavery of sin and asked me to join Keith and Stewey in a song of praise with a chorus that went, 'Thank you, thank you, thank you Jesus/ Thank you for the way you feed us.' Radio St Helena followed on the same wavelength and brought the news that three men in Jamestown had today been found guilty of driving a car while they had too much alcohol in their bloodstream and Mrs Yon had lost her blue coat so if anyone found it could they please return it to her.

On the first morning we drank more orange tea and stared out at the bare patch of earth on which this house was built, a ragged eucalyptus in the foreground and the wide sweep of the Atlantic Ocean beyond it, while on all sides there was the clustering companionship of other bungalows that also clung to this stretch of hillside. The mina birds shrieked at each other and stalked about with the rather malevolent determination of eaters of carrion. A *Chuck and Chew* lorry drove noisily up the road, collecting black rubbish bags as it went, and someone in the bungalow immediately below us was playing loud Country and Western music.

Nothing had prepared me for all this gypsy-brash modernity. Back in England, I had asked several people to tell me about St Helena as they had known it, but no one I spoke to had been there for ten, twenty, even thirty years, and within that time there had been many changes. Napoleon had expected the luxury of fruit trees and rich forests and instead he found himself living in that desolate land called Deadwood Plain. I had expected donkeys and the occasional antique car crawling along in a haze of exhaust fumes, but there are hardly any working donkeys left and most of the old cars had quite recently been dumped in the bay at Jamestown to make an artificial reef of rusting metal and disintegrating upholstery. I had expected a lot of singing and dancing in people's houses in the evening, and visits to the local cinema with the audience roaring and shouting when the villain was being dangerous or the hero was in love, but the cinema has been turned into a shop that sells plastic goods shipped over from Brazil, and all that sociable noise has been swept away by the video machines that keep everyone staring silently in their own front rooms, and they have become ashamed of the old songs which do not have the rhythm and the confidence of Country and Western music.

One day I sat in the dim light of the Government Archive Department in Jamestown, talking to a man who has worked here for more than forty years, mending the pages of books and manuscripts that have been chewed up by the termites or blotched and crumpled by the damp, and answering letters that are mostly from people anxious to trace some distant family connection with Napoleon's island. He said it did make him sad to see how much had changed in recent years, but he thought that perhaps his sadness was tangled up with the fact of growing old, and if he missed the dancing he also missed the energy to want to dance any more. In a way it didn't really matter because the memory of how things had been would die with him and people like him, and the new generation would not need to know that anything had been lost.

The archivist said I had come ten years too late. Ten years ago there were hardly any cars and very many donkeys and people were poor but they still had fruit trees in their gardens. When he was a boy there had been enough sand in Jamestown bay to play football there at low tide, but it had been suctioned away to be used in making concrete blocks, until one day it became apparent that there was no sand left at all.

I asked him if any islander had ever written about this place and he said yes, there had been a man who had made an entry in his diary for every day of his adult life, and he would stop people in the street and say, 'Do you know what happened here, twenty, thirty years ago, on this same date?' and then he would produce his diary for that year and read out the entry. But when he died there was no trace of any of his papers; perhaps he had destroyed them himself.

It would seem as if St Helena has never had a very tight hold on its own history. Many of the local people presume that if something is valuable then it will be taken away from them and shipped off to England or elsewhere, and if they can keep it then it must be worthless. They have thrown out their blue and white china with its wonderful bestiary of images and replaced it with items made out of plastic, aluminium and Pyrex and they have found a modern equivalent for their heavy wooden furniture. Every four years a new governor arrives and is inaugurated in a flurry of colonial ceremony and within that short space of time he can, if it pleases him, play at his leisure with the sensation of being a king. And there are others beneath him, a shifting hierarchy of experts and officials who can all make their mark by deciding what should or should not be done with the potato fields, the streams, the houses, the people.

I very much wanted to visit Plantation House, and since we were living nearby I walked there one Sunday afternoon, away from the bungalows and the new roads and through a beautiful forest of cedars and cactuses and groves of giant bamboo, with little doves calling to each other across the silence. The trees gave way to a clearing in bright sunlight with low stone houses painted in pink and blue and a pig-pen made out of flattened oil drums with 'Welcome Prince Andrew' written on one side in big brush strokes. A path led through a gate and a rather neglected vegetable garden and out on to the lawn of the Governor's residence. In the distance there was the house looking exactly as I had imagined it, and near to where I was standing there was the two-hundred-year-old tortoise who had failed to meet Napoleon, wheezing and sighing with his old man's tongue and his one blind eye.

I walked across the lawn, past flowerbeds and tennis courts, and rang a shining bell at the front door. Through a spotlessly clean window I could see a frail and ancient individual who was intent on polishing a large table and who looked exactly like my idea of how a governor should look. A young man in uniform opened the door, but only slightly, and said that if I wanted to see around the house then I would have to contact the Governor's private secretary and make an appointment.

So I telephoned the secretary on the next day and rather crossly he asked me why, since I was writing a book about Napoleon, I wanted to look around the house that had been occupied by Sir Hudson Lowe. He said it was most inconvenient, but if it was really necessary then I could telephone again in three days' time and he would see what could be arranged.

I suppose it was unnecessary in a way; walking from one elegant room to the next, British royalty on the walls, soft carpets on the floors, but still it would have been odd to leave the island without seeing that house from the inside. The man who looked like a governor was still busy with his polishing and he smiled and bowed and said he had worked here since he was a boy, thank you ma'am. I was surprised to see Napoleon in the library, done larger than life in black and white and looking angry and ill as he hung beside the marble fireplace and stared out at the row upon row of books on the shelves, many of them history books ancient and modern that had originally been sent to keep him busy at Longwood. This library had been built when

Sir Hudson Lowe was in command here, but there was no portrait of him on display so he was not given the opportunity of answering Napoleon's stare, like those bodiless trophies of wild animals that can snarl at each other across an enclosed space, glass eyes confronting glass eyes.

It is difficult to know what to think of Sir Hudson Lowe. As soon as Napoleon was safely buried he announced rather grandly that he forgave his prisoner everything, and his sudden and unexpected departure from life into death filled him with deep remorse and regret. He began to make friendly overtures to the French at Longwood, and on 12 May, after he and Lady Lowe had enjoyed their tour of Napoleon's rooms and inspection of his possessions, he invited Montholon, Bertrand and Madame Bertrand to honour him with a visit to Plantation House. It is said that these three had by now shaken off their gloom and despondency and had been transformed into the most 'social, cheerful and communicative beings', and since everyone got on so well and so courteously at this first meeting, there followed a number of lunches and supper parties to which many of the island's notables were also invited. Lady Lowe was very pleased to be told how Napoleon had once prepared and dressed himself with great care when he heard that she was expected to visit him in his garden at Longwood. Lowe wrote a letter to England in which he described the nature of his relationship with the deceased: 'several conversations had taken place with me, one in particular when Bonaparte had treated me with the most marked courtesy and distinction, the others rather stormy, *but always on his part alone*' (Lowe Papers, 20,240).

Meanwhile the French were busy preparing for their imminent departure. They had been told that they could all travel back to Europe on a cattle freighter called *The Camel* which had arrived at Jamestown on 10 May and was due to

sail on 24 May, and they had been provided with forty
large packing cases in which they could store all the things
that they wanted to take with them. They packed away the
white muslin curtains and wall hangings that had only just
been hung to make some of the rooms look more presentable, and they folded up the black draperies that had
covered the walls and ceilings when Napoleon was waiting
to be buried. They took almost everything that they had
brought with them from France or had acquired during
their stay on the island and they left behind almost
everything that had been provided for their use by the
British government. They obtained permission to take a
piano that did not belong to them and they left the wooden
aviary and the carriage that had been converted into a
funeral car.

The Camel's departure was delayed for a couple of days,
but on 26 May the cases, the servants and Napoleon's dog
Sambo, whose existence has never been spoken of before,
are all put on board, while Montholon, the Bertrands, the
priest Vignali and the young doctor Antommarchi are
invited to take part in a final dinner at Plantation House.
They enjoy a 'brilliant and magnificent evening' and on the
following morning their host and hostess accompany them
down to the harbour and wish them a safe journey home.
At three o'clock the ship sets sail, turning the wheels of the
last six years full circle as the island's steep sides recede
into the distance, the transition from dusk to night
becomes less abrupt and the stars slowly reposition themselves in the night sky.

Sir Hudson Lowe remains on St Helena for a further two
months. During this time he is able to supervise a much
more thorough examination of what has been left behind
by the French and what value can be placed on it. Long lists
are drawn up in which furniture and household goods,
books and maps, teaspoons and nutcrackers, garden
spades and buckets are all itemised, and all the new wood

that has been used in the construction of Longwood New House is measured and valued per foot. Lowe makes a note of the fact that numerous pieces of furniture are 'mostly in a very bad state, having been in use for more than five years, and not well taken care of whilst they were in use', and he proposes that the best thing to do with them is to dispose of them at a public auction. However, there are certain items that he would like to keep for himself, either, as he says, 'as relics of so extraordinary a Character', or, as he also says, 'not on account of any past interest attached to them, but because they would be useful to he and his family on their passage home'. So he arranges for eleven packing cases to be made by a carpenter, and into them goes Napoleon's big library table, his ink stand, the chairs he most often sat upon, the sofa he reclined on, the cups he drank from, the carpets he walked across. Mr Darling, who has been helping Lowe with the inventories, works out a valuation for all these items, 'because I am afraid that if I purchase them at the sale, they will go too high', and Lowe agrees to pay the British government the sum of £352 and 15 shillings for his entire collection of useful souvenirs.

For some reason the auction was delayed and Lowe was not able to take his eleven cases with him when he left the island in July 1821. He had arranged for them to be shipped over to England as soon as possible, but in his absence no one bothered to obey his instructions, and almost a year later the cases were still there at Plantation House, piled up in a cumbersome heap. The new Governor, General Walker, was eager to clear up all matters relating to General Bonaparte, and he decided to go ahead with the plans for the 'Sale by Auction of the Furniture, horses and etcetera belonging to the late Establishment at Longwood (the Property of Government)' which was to take place on 6 May 1822, and 'every subsequent Monday and Thursday, until the whole is disposed of'. While preparing for the sale

Governor Walker came across the eleven cases, broke them open and examined their contents. He realised immediately that he would like to be the owner of this particular selection of battered furniture and relics, and so he arranged to buy everything a second time over, and before anyone could object, he packed the entire collection on to the next boat bound for the British Isles and had it sent to his family home in Scotland.

CHAPTER XXI

'Let us go gently, gentlemen,' said Don
Quixote, 'for there are no birds this
year in last year's nests.'

Cervantes, *Don Quixote*

St Helena has left me with an unfamiliar aspect of sadness
which confronts me whenever I turn my head to look at the
memories I have of the few weeks I spent there. I suppose
this has something to do with knowing, almost with a
certainty, that I shall never go on that long sea journey
again, so the island is excluded from whatever pattern my
life might follow in the future; but this is not the heart of
the problem. You can carry the image of a place in your
mind in just the same way as you can carry the image of a
person long dead; the fact of not being able to return to that
particular connection does not need to matter. No, the
problem with St Helena is that the island and many of its
inhabitants seem to be permeated with despair. There it is,
a little steep-sided rock in the middle of a vast ocean; the
weather is mild and the trees are green, the sea is thick with

fish and all sorts of fruit and vegetables could grow in the soil; the days are quiet and the nights are dark; the faces of the people are gentle and their manners are hospitable and you cannot help but think that this might be quite a happy place if only it could break from the habit of its own history. Instead the island has grown accustomed to serving as a prison; the rules and regulations that were needed to turn it into a factory under the control of the East India Company metamorphosed into the ones that were used to guard the Emperor and the descendants of those same rules and regulations can be seen today, dressed in modern clothes, but still controlling every aspect of people's lives.

St Helena is one of the last outposts of the British Empire and it seems that it has been turned into a training ground for bureaucrats, a ship of fools that is being swung in slow circles by the government experts and officials who are sent out from England in droves and are given the freedom to do what they think is best during the few months or years of their stay. The islanders themselves have no control over the destiny of their little country; they are dependent on the financial subsidies that are sent to help them and they must accept whatever use that money is put to. They hold a British passport that gives them no right to settle in England or to go anywhere else; wages are low and the cost of living is as high as it was in Napoleon's time, and since almost every job is a government job, you would be wise to keep quiet and not complain about any apparent injustice.

There was once a man, so I was told, who tried to set up a local fishing industry with good wages and a canning factory, but he was accused of being a foreign spy and after his enterprise had closed down the fishing rights were sold to the Japanese who can now sieve all life out of the water for miles around. Until a few years ago, so I was also told, there was a good potato field over at Longwood and it had always provided enough potatoes for the entire island until an agricultural expert came and insisted that the crop would grow better somewhere else and a housing expert organised the erection of new houses on the old field so that now all potatoes have to be imported from South Africa. As I pause to think of the many things I was told by people who had no reason to lie or to exaggerate my head begins to swim and I can hear myself ranting with indignation, echoing perhaps some of the anger of Dr O'Meara or Count de Las Cases, or so many of the other people whose dead voices I have grown accustomed to listening to.

Because it was difficult to buy fresh fruit or vegetables on the island and anything you could buy was always so expensive, our neighbours, with the kindness of poor people, brought us daily gifts from their gardens and from the gardens of friends or relatives: small sour oranges, a mango from a tree that still flourished in Jamestown, a watery yam that turned a terrible grey colour when it was boiled and fried, a few tomatoes, a bunch of flowers in a china vase. When the time came to leave I felt as if I was betraying these people simply by being able to go away and now almost a year later I try to keep the tenuous thread of communication intact, writing letters that can take two months to reach their destination, or even longer if the ship is delayed as it has been in recent weeks. One woman writes to ask if my two children still remember the old tortoise who lives on the lawn in front of Plantation House. A new governor will be coming soon, she says, and she is surprised we are still thinking of Lemon Valley, it is too hot to walk there now in this heat; the boat has been held up at Ascension Island with engine trouble; food is getting more expensive but they had some nice tuna fish and everyone is well thank God. Perhaps one day we might come back for a holiday, never give up hope.

Some of the people I talked to on St Helena were filled

with anger, but perhaps it is easier to try to withdraw into a waking dream, with hope kept on a short rein, staring at the clouds as they move above the mountains, gazing out at the horizon for the sign of an approaching ship. In many parts of that strange island it looks as though the business of living had suddenly been interrupted; as if a whistle of command had been blown and, obedient and unquestioning, people had deserted their homes and their gardens, their fortresses and their look-out posts, leaving the evidence of their lives scattered in discarded heaps. Whatever was left behind – a solitary fruit tree standing close to a wall; a thin wild cat; a woman in a house on a bare mountainside – seemed to be held in a trance, waiting for the word or the kiss that would break the spell.

Lemon Valley was where the sailors had once come to collect thousands of lemons, cutting down entire trees festooned with fruit and carrying them to ships at anchor in the little bay, and now the steep path to the sea is hemmed in by cactus and bare rocks and you come across the ruins of old buildings, the ground scattered with broken bottles rainbowed with age; rusting chains and spikes fixed into rocks and walls; pieces of prettily painted china embedded in the earth as if people had danced on their own plates and fine dishes. There was no way of knowing if this or that skeleton of a house had been a military base in Napoleon's time, or a quarantine station a bit later, or a farm dating back to the first days of settlement. There were old and new graffiti on some of the walls and a little stream had been partially channelled into a plastic pipe that led to a tap fixed to an upright post, standing forlorn among the boulders by the sea. I wondered if Fernando Lopez might have lived here near this stream; there were several caves that could have given shelter to him and his cockerel. Once, on our way back up the path, we were watched by a pale donkey who maintained his shy distance but kept calling to us with a mournful laugh and that made me think of him. I asked a man who worked in the Jamestown hospital if he had heard of Fernando Lopez and he said oh yes, everyone knows about him, he was a black slave who committed some terrible crime in Portugal and he was mutilated and sent to St Helena as a punishment although in the end he was allowed to return home.

Rupert's Bay, on the sheltered side of the island and not far from Jamestown, is a wide valley reaching down to the sea and here there is an electricity generating plant, an abandoned fish-drying shed and a few poor houses with children playing in the dust of the single street. There are cannons and heavy chains rusting among boulders and in a patch of black volcanic sand I found a metal soldier's button and a piece of pottery that had been carefully chipped into a circle the size of a coin with the head of a unicorn on it. During the 1840s and 1850s St Helena was used as a sort of clearing house for thousands of freed slaves taken from captured slaving ships and Rupert's Bay was the depot where these people were unloaded. Those who died were buried in mass graves like the one they unearthed recently when they were making the foundations for the electricity plant; those who did not die were offered a passage to the West Indies, or if they refused to make another long journey, they could choose to stay here.

There are many half-forgotten and unlikely burial sites on the island. We came across a broken eighteenth-century tombstone on a rocky ridge where it would seem impossible to dig a hole deep enough to contain a coffin. There was another, for Mr Butcher and his wife, with a carving of an axe where you might expect an angel's winged head or a skull, almost overgrown by a clump of giant bamboos in the middle of a dark wood. A few weeks ago I had a letter from an Englishman whose distant ancestor's grave had been hemmed in and eventually shattered by the spread of the flax bushes on a hillside.

The landscape of Sandy Bay is so bleak and forbidding that it looks as if nothing could ever have grown here since the beginning of time, and yet this is where the thick forests of ebony were once to be found, and you can still come across the blackened stump of a root or a branch amongst the bare stone and barren earth. I have seen a photograph of a single fig tree that used to grow near the sea wall; it had reached a great size by growing horizontally just a few inches above the ground so as to avoid the battering of the wind, but someone cut it down during the first stage of a reforestation programme that never got very far.

There is a long twisted branch of Sandy Bay ebony propped up against a wall in a government building in Jamestown; a card tied to it with a piece of pink ribbon explains what it is and where it has come from. In that same hallway there is the broken lid of a wooden box carved with an inscription which says it contains '38 pickles for the Establishment at Longwood', and a pottery olive jar which 'might possibly be from one of the captured slave ships which were destroyed by the great rollers in February 1846'. In a far corner there is a small stone column with a face carved on it that looks like the face of Christ on the Turin shroud; a hollowed-out socket at the top of this column was being used to hold cigarette butts and a few nails. I asked several people where it had come from and how old it was, but no one seemed to know anything about it. Perhaps the oddest of all these floating remnants of the past was a cardboard box in the Archive Department, filled with something that looked like very old cornflakes. It was the earliest record book relating to the capture of the slaving ships and the legal proceedings against the slavers, but the termites which had been brought in with one of these ships had eaten their way through the evidence.

Two years after Napoleon's death, in 1823, it was decided that the best thing to do with his empty house was to turn it once again into a farm building. The decision was made by the new Governor, General Walker, who considered this the 'most necessary and useful function' that the building could be made to serve, and so it was quickly adapted to its new identity. The bathroom, empty now of its dark bath, and the two bedrooms stripped of beds and furniture, were turned into stables for carthorses; pigs were kept in what had been the kitchen and they could wander freely in the enclosed area of the kitchen courtyard where once Dr O'Meara had watched the rats frolic. The billiard table had been removed to Plantation House and the room was used as storage for animal feeds. The ceiling of the dining-room, still with its flamboyant red and gold wallpaper, was broken open so that a grain chute could be installed there. The drawing-room became the heart of the building and it was here that agricultural machinery was kept, with a threshing machine for corn against one wall and a beet-slicing machine positioned between the two windows. Before leaving the house General Bertrand tore a strip of wallpaper from the wall and marked the spot with a drawing of a crown, and he also took a small piece of floorboard with him as well. I am looking now at a contemporary drawing of that room, with those two heavy pieces of industrial machinery, the thresher and the beet-cutter, standing there like insects guarding their territory against intruders. The door into the next room has gone, the ceiling has gone, exposing the rafters, the familiar grey light of dereliction and neglect is coming in through the windows, but you can see the mark on the wall and the hole in the floor. I could imagine myself going to Longwood at that time, walking across a garden that was now a waste land, up the stone steps, through the unlocked front door, its paint cracked and peeling, and into the billiard-room where the wallpaper has been pulled off in strips and the walls are covered with names and dates and the thoughts and comments inscribed by the many visitors who came to St Helena and visited Longwood and the tomb in the years immediately after Napoleon's death:

On entering a dirty court-yard, and quitting our horses we were shown by some idlers into a square building which once contained the bedroom, sitting room and bath of the Empereur des François. The partitions and floorings are now thrown down and torn up . . . I entered a small chamber with two windows looking towards the North . . . The apartment is now occupied by a threshing machine. We were conducted onwards to a large room which formerly contained a billiard table and whose front looks out upon a little latticed verandah . . . The whitewashed walls are scored with the names of every nation; and the paper of the ceiling has been torn off in strips as holy relics. (Captain Mundy, vol. II, pp. 355–6)

The garden fell apart even more quickly than the house. The peach trees, the roses, the éternelles and the passion-flowers put up no resistance once they were without water and attention; the earth ramparts and the sunken paths slid and crumbled; the grotto collapsed in upon itself, the tea-house and the latticed walkway were broken and lost. The fish pool that had been Napoleon's first metal bath dried up, but survived more or less intact, while all the other tanks and channels for carrying water disappeared. Farm animals wandered at their leisure through most of the garden, although one area was enclosed and used for growing potatoes.

The grave also went through its own metamorphoses. In 1824 Mr Torbett sent a written complaint to a government official, saying that his land had become

a thoroughfare for persons desirous of visiting the Tomb, of the said General Bonaparte, and the public conceiving the lands to be a thoroughfare, converge on the land and come through these premises at all Hours, from which causes the Gate Posts have been taken out of the Ground, the Trees broken down, and by which means the Cattle and Horses have access to the grounds in cultivation, much to the injury of the said Master Torbett. (Lowe Papers, 20,229)

The original guard of armed soldiers had been ordered to leave after a few months and in their place there was an old English sergeant and his wife who lived in a hut a few paces from the tomb. The sergeant had a little patch of cultivated land where he grew cuttings from the willow trees which he sold to visitors, putting each rooted twig into a wine bottle or a pickling bottle filled with water from the spring. It was also possible to buy a cup or a bottle of spring water and local people came to the tomb to sell items of food to strangers. The metal fence that Sir Hudson Lowe had arranged to have fixed around the tomb had a couple of its railings removed so that people could stand on top of Napoleon, and could if they wished carve their initials into the stones that covered him. It was said that the old sergeant was well-informed about his subject; his wife boasted that he had read it 'all in a book in print', and he would explain to each new arrival, 'Here's the railing round the ground, and there's the paling round the tomb, eight feet deep, six feet long, and three feet wide.' Before leaving, visitors were requested to make a financial contribution and to write an entry in the visitors' book which he kept in the sentry box, pen and ink ready.

I find it quite easy to imagine Longwood as it appeared during those years of its neglect. I can make my way through rooms darkened by dirty glass and cobwebs, filled with the smell of dust and animals, conscious of the presence of the wind outside pulling and pushing at the structure of the decaying building. I can look at the words written on damp walls and cut into the wood of a door, and notice a place where a bath must have been, or a bed or a picture, but always there is the clear knowledge that the place is deserted and its history belongs to the past. With the tomb it must have been very different. Hundreds, even, so they say, thousands, of visitors came to look at Napoleon's grave, making the rough track that led down to the road trampled and muddy, while the willow trees were torn to pieces by those who wanted to take something alive away with them. The mud, the broken trees and broken fences can be ignored quite easily, but what remains strangely disquieting is the image of the people who enter that metal cage above the coffin and are preoccupied with the business of carving the date and their own name into the flagstones.

CHAPTER XXII

'Ay, every inch a king.'

Shakespeare, *King Lear*

Today is 14 January 1991. Tomorrow there is the possibility that a war might break out across the countries of the Middle East, and then might spread further, tearing through people's lives and changing their understanding of the world. Sometimes it can seem as if the future has already been decided upon; as if the extent and the nature of the confusion that is now heading towards us is there like the map of a carefully-charted landscape, hanging on a wall behind a thin curtain. And meanwhile here I sit, on this day as on many others, staring out of the window and back into my own memory, trying to find a hook that will pull me towards the events I want to describe; searching for something that will help me to recognise certain features in the territory of this story about an emperor and an island in a distant time that has been and gone long ago.

There is not very much left to tell. I have reached the stage when Napoleon is to be dug up out of his grave in the Valley of the Tomb in order that he might be taken back in triumph to France. Nineteen years have passed since his heavy coffins were lowered with ropes and pulleys into the deep hole in the earth and sealed off with bricks, slabs of stone and cement. Soon the whole process must be set into reverse: lifting off the stones one by one, breaking through the layers of cement reinforced with bands of metal, forcing the lids off the coffins and finally being confronted by the sight of a dead man, there at the centre of it all like the kernel of a nut.

I was once taken to see a mummified saint who was lying in the crypt of a church somewhere on the east coast of Ireland. I can still see the steps going down into a peaty darkness that shimmered with pools of candlelight and I can see the body of the saint as I first distinguished him or her, stretched out on a platform, thin and brown, partially wrapped in sheets of brown cloth. I was about eight years old and just tall enough to stand on a level with the face and stare at something that was unmistakably human but was also like the twisted branch of a tree that happened to have the features of a person. Someone told me to take hold of the hand and shake it because that would bring me good luck, but shake it very gently since the arm was loose in its socket and in danger of breaking off. Tentatively and with the seriousness of childhood, I took the hard and polished brown hand in my own, raised it up a little way and lowered it down again, and now it is the memory of this distant encounter that returns to me as I watch the exhumation of Napoleon and stand in a tent with the rain beating down outside, staring at his mummified body dressed in military costume, the hands and face pale and hard as wood, the silver of the buttons and medals tarnished to the colour of copper.

A number of the people who had lived with Napoleon

on St Helena came back to witness the exhumation. General Gourgaud was there, quarrelling and complaining as bitterly as ever, but now with a much heavier body, a red face and a grey beard. Count de Las Cases was unable to come since he was entirely blind and near to the end of his life, but his son Emmanuel came to represent him and to be confronted by his own memories of the time when he had slept with his father in the little attic room of the Pavilion and had copied out page after page of Napoleon's account of recent history. The two priests, Buonovita and Vignali, were both dead, one of old age, the other killed in a duel; Dr Antommarchi had died in Cuba and Dr O'Meara had died in London. Count Montholon was living in exile and could not join the group, but General Bertrand was able to come: a frail widower who brought with him the faded uniforms he had worn when he was on the island. He was accompanied by his son Arthur who had been born on St Helena in 1817 and was presented to Napoleon as 'the first Frenchman to come to Longwood without a permit'.

Many of the original servants made the journey as well: Marchand, who was now a wealthy and well-established figure; St Denis, who had watched Napoleon so closely, sleeping on the floor beside his bed and trying to help steer him through the monotony of each day; Pierron the pastrycook who had made palaces out of spun sugar; Archambault the groom who had lifted up his master's head when Dr Burton was making a plaster cast of the back of the skull; Noverazz the third valet who had been very ill when Napoleon was dying. With them came the third son of King Louis Philippe, the Prince de Joinville, and Count Rohan-Chabot who was to act as the supervisor for all the dealings between the French and the English.

They set out from France in July 1840, travelling in two boats, *La Belle Poule* and *La Favorite*, and bringing with them everything considered necessary for the funeral of an emperor. A mortuary chapel had been set up in *La Belle*

Poule; the walls were hung with black velvet studded with golden stars and silver tassels, with a glass candelabra hanging from the ceiling so that as the ship moved over the waves the room had a fairground glitter of reflected lights. There was an empty coffin made out of polished ebony and shaped like a stone sarcophagus, with NAPOLEON written in shining letters, a gold star covering the lock, and inside this coffin, framed by the laurels and arabesques of heroes there were the words:

Napoleon
Emperor and King
Died at St Helena
May 5 1821

A stone cenotaph stood in one corner surmounted by the imperial crown, with paintings done in the Roman style showing stiff-bodied human images representing Justice, History, Religion and the Legion of Honour. And, ready to be draped over the coffin once it contained the corpse, a rich pall of purple velvet trimmed with ermine and decorated with swarms of golden bees and crowned golden eagles.

The journey took a long time. They were three months at sea, stopping for several days at Madeira and Tenerife, for three weeks at Bahia on the coast of Brazil, and spending six days floating without movement when the wind deserted them in the Doldrums. Then on 7 October 1840 they had their first sighting of St Helena, wrapped in a thick blanket of mist and dark clouds. They approached the island from Sandy Bay and travelled round past George Island where the clay for Napoleon's death mask might have come from, and past that bleak mound of rock called the Barn, where according to one man in the company they could see the Emperor staring out from the line of the rocks. I cannot help doubting that they really saw that familiar face in the gathering darkness; throughout this visit the island itself, as well as the sun, the wind, the rain, even the stars in the sky, were all expected to cooperate in paying homage to a dead man who had been left on his own for so long but was now coming home.

The new Governor of the island, an old man called Major-General Middlemore, had been warned well in advance about the arrival of his foreign guests and so there was plenty of time to make sure that on this occasion the English would honour the French with all possible courtesy. Fine rooms were made ready in the castle with a banqueting table set out for the evenings' entertainments. The best house in Jamestown was reserved to receive any extra visitors, a grand welcome was prepared at the quay and there were horses and carriages, uniformed guards and liveried servants, all waiting to be told what was expected of them. And so for a second time a little group of people came ashore, passed along familiar streets and were faced by a crowd of onlookers and soldiers, officials and their wives some of whom they could still recognise. Emmanuel de Las Cases describes walking through Jamestown: 'I contemplated everything slowly, hardly able to believe my eyes, experiencing what one feels when waking from a dream. My memories were as alive and real as if our captivity had only ceased the day before.' (Martineau (1976), p. 109)

It was decided that Napoleon would be lifted up out of his grave on 15 October, exactly twenty-five years since he was first confronted by the dark silhouette of the island that lay ahead of him. Most of the necessary preparations had been made in advance: the track down to the tomb had been widened and cleared, and the area all around it had been tidied up so that the marks of the trampling feet of men and animals had been erased. Fences were mended, flowers were planted, and a group of soldiers was stationed there along with the old guard and his wife and the other 'keepers of the Tomb', to make sure that the atmosphere of the place was not disturbed. A sturdy carriage was obtained, stripped of its top and turned into a wheeled platform that would be able to support the immense weight of Napoleon within the layers of wood and metal that contained him. Two tents were erected near to the tomb, one to serve as a shelter and storage place for the tools and equipment needed for the excavation and for the workers while they were busy with their task; the other, decorated rather incongruously in blue and white stripes like the marquee of a garden party, was to be used to hold the coffins while they were opened up and their contents verified.

On 9 October, after some formal visits at the castle and Plantation House, the French made their first pilgrimage to Napoleon's resting place. One man describes how he saw the grave standing in the dappled shade of the willow trees, but there were only two willows left by now and one of them was dead and lying on its side like a beached whale, while the other had been stripped of all its small branches and leaves so that its shadow must have been rather austere. While some men stood in silence, staring at the fences and the stones, others became very busy as people sometimes do when they are confronted by an emotion. The Prince gave orders for the dead willow to be immediately hoisted on to a handcart and taken to James-town where it could be chopped up and distributed among the French sailors. The groom Archambault managed to obtain a piece of this willow which eventually made its way to a museum in Paris; it now stands in the company of one of the spikes from the railings which looks like the blunt spearhead from some ancient battle. Arthur Bertrand collected sprigs from the geraniums which he hoped were the same ones that his mother had planted, and the Prince collected a bunch of forget-me-nots, a flower that I don't remember seeing anywhere on the island. As they left and began to make their way towards Longwood a wind was already blowing and it began to rain.

I watch this group of men walking towards the house that many of them had known so well. They enter the garden and find traces of the paths and flowerbeds that they helped to dig and lay out; the stump of a tree that they think was the tree by which they once sat; a drinking trough for cattle that must be the ornamental pool shaped like a half moon that was supposed to hold fish. They enter the house and move through damp and empty rooms in which they themselves are the ghosts who have broken through the boundary of time. Marchand leads the way and explains to the Prince what it was that each room once contained, peopling the haunted dereliction with furniture, ornaments, human activity. Maybe it was on this occasion, and not in 1821 as I had first thought, that the old Bertrand, dressed in his faded uniform, pulls off a strip of paper from the wall in the drawing-room and makes a little drawing of a crown to mark the place where his master's bed once stood.

The days go by occupied by small social activities: visits to certain houses and people, meetings with officials. The heavy sarcophagus is heaved up to the tomb on the hearse and placed in readiness in the blue and white tent. Little groups of French sailors are given permission to go to Longwood and the tomb and they come back with armfuls of trophies: plants and flowers, fragments of stone and woodwork, sacks filled with earth. Finally on the night of 14 October the party of Frenchmen makes its way to the tomb. Soldiers are standing on guard all around the area to keep intruders away, torches and lanterns light up the darkness and the rain, the excavators are ready to begin their work. The first thing they do is to dig up all the bulbous plants that still remain in the soil – the lilies that grow so well in this climate – and these are piled up in a battered white heap to be divided later. They tear down one side of the metal railings that Napoleon had always hated, and they heave up the stonework in which they had been set. With hooks and hoists they lift the covering flagstones with all the initials and dates of strangers cut into them, and then a group of English soldiers armed with pickaxes and shovels begins the work of excavation. They dig through six feet of heavy clay, shining and slippery in the rain, and at three in the morning they reach the first layer of cement. They are able to smash through this without much problem but then they are confronted by the second layer, ten inches thick and made out of rough stones matted together with iron tendons. While one group starts battering at this fortified lid that was designed to protect Napoleon from intruders, a second team sets to work digging a trench beside the vault, so that if necessary they can reach their goal that way. By eight o'clock in the morning, with the valley enveloped in a thick mist and the rain still falling, they reach the single slab of stone that lies directly above Napoleon. Two rings are fixed into this, just as they were nineteen years previously, and before they begin to work the hoists the English captain in charge of the operations announces, like a general about to shatter the gates of a besieged city, 'Gentlemen, hardly six inches separate us at this moment from Napoleon's coffin.' (Aubry, p. 602) Up goes the stone and there in the vault they can see the container of dark mahogany wood that had once been somebody's dining-room table. Everyone removes their hats, a French priest sprinkles holy water and recites the words of Psalm 130, 'Out of the depths have I cried unto thee, O Lord', while three men clamber down into the vault to examine the state of the coffin. One islander, a man called George Bennett, manages to pass through the ring of soldiers in the mist, and just before he is discovered and chased out of this circle of concentration, he has time to see 'a great commotion, and men were hauling at ropes through a pulley hanging from a triangle erected over the grave. In another moment up came the coffin, shining and wet, and there it hung, like that of Mahommet, between heaven and earth.' (Bennett, Pt. 10)

The coffin is carried to the tent and its outer casing is stripped away to be shared among everyone present. The rest is lowered into the black sarcophagus and then the process of moving still closer to the corpse begins. They cut through the screws and lift off one lid; through a layer of lead, a layer of wood, and there they reach the final shell, covered with a white, powdery growth caused by the process of oxidization. They cut through the soldered edges of the tin, lifting it back to reveal whatever it is that lies beneath it. And here, if words could be used like music, the orchestra would now fall silent and from out of that silence a single instrument, or a human voice, high and cold, would return to the simple outline of the musical theme.

The body of Napoleon is covered with fragments of white satin that have fallen from the lid above him. Very carefully, a French doctor lifts this covering, moving from the feet upwards, with all those urgent faces gathered round and staring down into the white bed as if it was a cradle containing the mystery of a newborn child. First the familiar black riding boots that have split open to reveal white toes breaking out from the leather like the shoots of bulbs emerging from the earth. The legs in their white britches, the hat on the thigh and the tarnished silver eagle from the dish containing the heart growing up between the thighs; the hands white, hard and perfect. Everyone notices that the nails have grown since the lid was closed. The jacket of the Chasseur du Gard, still green with a red lining and the colours perhaps less faded than the old clothes Bertrand is wearing for the occasion. The medals and buttons tarnished to that strange mottled purple and bronze of neglected silver. (It is said that the star of the Legion of Honour on its sash was still shining brightly, although this might be only to please the people who wish to see it shine.) The face pale, three teeth showing where the lip has pulled back, the skin grey where the stubble of a new beard first started to grow. The eyelids hard and firmly closed with no chance of seeing a flicker of movement such as I thought I saw on the eyes of the unconscious Spanish general whose image first helped me to imagine Napoleon on the island of St Helena.

There, lying between the Emperor's legs, and pushed in around him in his satin bed, are all the objects that were provided to keep him company in his isolation: a collection of coins from France and Italy, minted with his own impassive face, in case he needed to buy anything, or find a way of explaining the position he had once held in the world of men; the knife and fork to cut his meat; the silver sauceboat; the plate on which an Englishman's name had been scratched; and perhaps, if indeed there was enough room, a loaf of bread and a bottle of water for hunger and for thirst.

Once again the doctor in the group was too professionally keen and wanted to lift the body out of the coffin so that he could examine it more thoroughly in the name of science, but Gourgaud with his red face and his anger intervened and it was agreed that Napoleon should be left alone and sealed up as quickly as possible before the action of the air destroyed the impression of immortality. So the doctor contented himself with feeling the unexpected hardness of the body, the legs, the belly, the hand, the eyelid, and then with a final parting look from this gathering of Englishmen and Frenchmen, the Emperor was again wrapped into layers of wood and metal, the key in the golden lock of his sarcophagus was turned and he was ready to make his slow progress back to the port of Jamestown.

CHAPTER XXIII

'I wish *I* could manage to be glad!' the
Queen said. 'Only I can never
remember the rule. You must be very
happy, living in this wood, and being
glad whenever you like!'

Lewis Carroll, *Through the Looking Glass*

Although there is not much more to tell about the Emperor
and the island, I now find myself surrounded by an
ungainly collection of things that I still have not said, all
seeming to stare at me with baleful eyes as if this particular
image, or fact, or aspect of a landscape, would explain
something that otherwise could never be understood. I
have been going through some of my notebooks and from
them I have assembled a list. It includes a dance in a
concrete building overlooking Sandy Bay; a man with
almost no voice who used to paint pictures of the island;
the butcher from his village and his house; the Sultan of
Zanzibar; the fishing trawler, the dolphins and the three
distant rainstorms that we saw on our way home just after
we had crossed the Equator, and, echoing through it all,
the remaining details of Napoleon's departure from St

Helena and what was left of him there, once he had gone.

I'll begin with the butcher. Exactly a year ago today he invited me to look around the abandoned house that had belonged to his family for many generations and in which he had been born and had spent his childhood. The last person to live there was a bachelor uncle who had worn a top hat and smoked *Romantico* Havana cigars with a lady in a red dress on the lid. But even while the uncle was in the house it was already falling down, with ivy growing through the broken panes of the windows and creeping with cautious fingers along the inside walls. The butcher stood in the room in which he had been born. The morning light filtered in through the overgrown windows and the metal bed on which his mother had lain during her labour was piled high with bundles of old newspapers. From the mist of his memory he told me how he had gone to the circus when he was a child and how the clown had pulled a false tail off a pony, giving him nightmares for years afterwards so that he would wake up screaming in this room. He showed me where the pigeons nested in the corridor and pointed to a heap of big flints that he had piled up on the lawn like some ancient burial mound because he liked the look of each one, even though some of them had been almost too heavy for him to carry on his back. Everything here, from the beautiful Elizabethan chimneys to the windows with their leaded panes, the washbasins and oval mirrors, the rose bushes and the dovecot, everything was on the edge of disappearing without trace and it would all be gone as soon as this old man was no longer there to think and talk about his past. And I had been asked to stand on the edge of his memories, so that for a moment I could look around me and see the house and its contents with his eyes.

Somehow that same sense of witnessing the passing of things was to be found everywhere on St Helena. I look back at the landscape of Sandy Bay and can see only naked earth where once there were trees. I look at a rich fold of land peopled with the white flowers of arum lilies, the hanging lace flowers of the petticoat tree, the fat well-fed trunks of the thorn trees, but I am distracted by a tumbled-down house, a new barbed-wire fence, the line of plastic piping which carries a trickle of spring water into the cistern of a flushing lavatory. I see myself walking to Lemon Valley, to Rupert's Bay, to Blue Hill; sitting in the wasteland that is still called Deadwood Plain, and each place is coloured by the knowledge of what it has been and how it has changed with the years. I see myself sitting with the old woman who was our neighbour, in her kitchen with its corrugated-iron walls painted a bright blue, the mina birds tapping on the roof and her dead husband's working boots standing side by side in the garden down by the fence near the road. I tell her what a nice china teapot she has and she immediately offers to give it to me, or would I like the milk jug, or the wooden cradle in the bedroom, the flowers in the garden? Each item is briefly transfigured while the spotlight shines on it, then falls back, quiet and colourless.

One night we went to a dance. We went with our two neighbours, the old woman and a young woman who was her friend, and the moon was full so that when the car came over the ridge above Sandy Bay we could see the whole sweep of the valley like a Wagnerian stage set, with the pyramid of Lot white and glistening, and far away near the edge of the sea, the column of his foolish wife who was never going to reach him. The dance was being held in a concrete courtyard in front of a little café, with neon strip-lighting competing with the moon, and tables and chairs set out and already occupied by a crowd of island people. All the different races of the world seemed to be gathered here: brown, black, yellow, white, in a café on the tip of a volcano in the middle of the Atlantic Ocean. When the music started the people began to dance, very formally with one hand holding the edge of a partner's waist and the other hand held high, old and young, round and round. The music was mostly loud and electric but there was one old man playing the fiddle, sitting there among the guitars, the drums and the red synthesiser, playing with his eyes closed and his head thrown back as if he was blind and there was no music apart from his own.

So that was the butcher and the dance and a few of the notes from the notebooks. Often these days I find myself shuffling the cards of all that I had expected from St Helena and all that I did find there, and then laying the cards out in front of me like a game of patience. Perhaps after all I should avoid describing the man with almost no voice who used to paint pictures of the island, and the Sultan of Zanzibar who was another of St Helena's prisoners, because they both lead towards a repetition of a pattern of thought, a matched sequence of cards. Let me return instead to the second funeral of Napoleon, with the rain still falling and the enormous coffin which now weighed over a ton, being dragged up the muddy track to the road by forty-three men and then heaved on to the platform of the hearse. The purple velvet with its bees and eagles is draped over the shining wood, and Marchand, Bertrand, Las Cases and Gourgaud each take hold of one embroidered corner. There are four horses to pull the hearse and twenty-four soldiers to push it up the slippery hill and to tug at the spokes whenever it gets stuck in the mud. A public notice has been displayed on all the notice boards of the island, saying that anyone who wishes to accompany the procession must dress themselves in 'Decent Mourning' and wait at Alarm Hill. And so when the hearse arrives at Alarm House at the top of the hill leading down to Jamestown, the road is lined with two files of soldiers and there once again is the population of St Helena, the slaves, the landowners and the shopkeepers, dressed in as much black material as could be found, ready to watch Napoleon making the first stage of his journey back to his own country, leaving the island that has held him for the last twenty-five years.

Now the soldiers have to pull on ropes attached to the hearse to stop it from hurtling forwards, and with great care they follow the windings of the road, looking out across at the Heart-Shaped Waterfall, down at The Briars and the pale roof of the Pavilion. They cross the little bridge that leads into Jamestown and go down a road that was soon to be renamed Napoleon Street, one of the poorest streets in a poor town where it was said to be 'impossible to pass . . . without being molested by drunkards, half naked prostitutes and stripped men fighting in the gutter' (Kitching, p. 59), but the soldiers have made sure that the streets are cleared of violence or rough behaviour. Throughout this stage of the journey the guns from the fortress at High Knoll are sending out their regular booming signals, and these are answered by the cannons of ships and rounds of artillery fired by soldiers. Two choirboys walk beside the French priest close to the hearse, singing a continuous clear-voiced chant for the dead man.

It takes them two hours to cover the short distance from the top of the hill to the quay. By then the rain has stopped and some people say that the sun was shining in a bright sky. All the shops and drinking houses in Jamestown are closed and all the ships in the bay are draped in black with black cloth wound around the masts and the rigging. The Prince de Joinville is there at the quay to welcome the procession and the island's Governor, General Middlemore, faces him and announces in the name of the British Government that he is handing over the body of the Emperor Napoleon. A longboat, draped with a silk tricolour flag, is moored at the quay, and with ropes and pulleys they hoist up the coffin, swing it out over the boat and lower it down. The guns are silent, funeral music is playing softly from *La Belle Poule* as if beckoning the Emperor to approach closer, and with the same group of four men standing at the four corners of the sarcophagus the boat is rowed out into deeper water and Napoleon is heaved up on to the deck of the ship. With more gunshot and cannon shot, with drums rolling and the sun setting into a red sea, the coffin is carried to a temporary resting place on the upper deck and there, by the light of lanterns in the darkness, the priest recites the prayers for the dead and, like the Corsican priest Vignali before him, prepares to watch beside the corpse until the dawn.

They set sail on the morning of 17 October. They take with them the slab of stone that had covered the tomb in the Vale of Geranium; sacks of earth; the shattered trunk of an old willow tree; rooting branches of willows and geraniums; quiet bulbs of lilies; the broken fragments of a mahogany coffin; pieces of doors and floorboards; strips of wallpaper; a birdcage made by a Chinese carpenter; a deep lead bath; a table, a footstool and a white sofa on which Napoleon used to lie in his private room, staring at the fire in the little grate.

During the first week of our return journey the sea was glassy calm. One day we saw a Russian fishing trawler: a huge grey ghost of a machine that turns everything it catches into a powder that is used for fertilising empty fields. It was on that same day that the dolphins came; as many as fifty of them all at once, leaping and dancing alongside the ship with an extraordinary vivid joy. One evening when we were on the same latitude as Dakar on the west coast of Africa, we seemed to be able to catch the scent of hot earth carried on the air across the expanse of ocean and along the length of the horizon we saw three separate rainstorms that suddenly erupted out of nowhere and hung motionless in the sky. Each one was a tangle of thick cloud with shafts of light and shadow cutting down into the water where the line of the rain was falling. As we watched and the sun began to set, the clouds became saturated with wild luminous colours: purple, yellow, grey and red, boiling in the distance.

CHAPTER XXIV

Make no noise, make no noise; draw
the curtains. So, so. We'll go to supper
i' th' morning.

Shakespeare, *King Lear*

If this story was being told as a piece of theatre, the curtains
would now close and open again to an empty stage and
one by one or in connected groups, all the characters who
have been involved would appear and bow to the
audience. First comes the Spanish colonel, miraculously
recovered from the effects of the car accident I witnessed
long ago; his hat placed firmly on his head, his eyes wide
open, his uniform immaculate. Next comes the island of St
Helena. I once played the part of Wall, in a school
production of *A Midsummer Night's Dream*, peering out
above a folded sheet of stiff paper on which bricks and
stones had been painted in bold strokes, and with that
memory in mind I can see the island advancing across the
stage: a human head poised on top of a dark steep-sided
mound, a papier mâché Christmas pudding decorated

with a few painted houses, roads and trees; it sways slightly as it walks forward and then goes over to one side to wait for the others. Now Fernando Lopez smiling through his twisted face, Betsy Balcombe laughing and pretty, and after her the French servants who were at Longwood, even the ones who left or died before the story had come to an end. An admiral, an ambassador, a shopkeeper, a soldier dressed in red; the round-faced Dr O'Meara holding hands with the reptilean Dr Antommarchi; the old priest Buonovita leaning on the shoulder of the young shepherd-priest Vignali, in whose hand I think I can see the dried holy relic that he took from the Emperor's corpse. I wonder if this is the moment when Sir Hudson Lowe should stride across the boards, or would it be better for him to wait until just before his prisoner arrives? Alternatively he could enter along with the French counts and generals: Las Cases hunched forward but with his eyesight restored; Bertrand with Madame Bertrand who is clasping a bunch of flowers similar to the ones she planted by the grave; Gourgaud looking less cross; Montholon and Madame Montholon, formal and dignified, and finally, in defiance of death and mummification, Napoleon himself; pale-faced, fat-bellied, walking on slippered feet to the centre of the stage. Then the island could bow to the Emperor and the Emperor could return an answering bow to the island, and the evening's entertainment would be over.

But because there is no stage to be filled or emptied like a conjurer's hat, I must attempt to bring things to a close in some other way; putting this or that item back in its correct place before leaving and shutting the door behind me. I remember once visiting the house in which I had lived for much of my childhood. I arrived at night, with no one knowing I was there, and for about an hour I sat on the lawn in the dark garden, watching the occasional flicker of human activity as someone walked behind a drawn curtain inside a familiar room, and it is that point of quiet valediction that I would now like to reach; stepping back from the story that has preoccupied me for so long and letting it drift away.

I had planned to make a second visit to France; to again go and stare at Napoleon in his shining sepulchre, but on this occasion to remember to look for the flagstones that used to cover his grave in St Helena and have since been cemented into a wall or a floor somewhere close to him. I could have gone to see the wooden aviary that provided shelter for a hen and a pheasant in the garden at Longwood, and that is now the principal exhibit in a museum in Boulogne. I could have gone to the Louvre and not been daunted by the crowds of strangers; threading my way through until I reached the cases containing the Sèvres plates Napoleon had always been so proud of, and there, close by, the ornate silver washbasin in which he washed, the mirror in which he saw himself, the alarm clock that had once belonged to Frederick the Great. Finally I could have visited the museum that is dedicated to the Emperor's return to France after an absence of twenty-five years: a painted frieze along a wall trying to give an impression of the thousands of people who poured out into the streets to welcome him, as if his arrival was the trumpet call for a last judgement. Eagles and bees, swords and crowns, silver, gold, purple and black, and I am sure that whenever the museum is open to the public, solemn and dignified music is playing, attenuating the events of a single day so that it would seem to be endless.

But instead of all this I decided to go and look at a painting of Napoleon that hangs in the Tate Gallery in London and at one of the visitors' books that used to be kept in the sentry's hut next to the tomb on the island, and is now to be found in a buff coloured envelope in the archive collection of the National Army Museum. The painting is a late work by J. M. W. Turner and it is called

War, the Exile and the Rock Limpet. On the day that I went it had been removed from its usual place on a wall in the main gallery and had been taken into a storeroom, and so I was led to it through heavy orange doors and into a subterranean catacomb filled with unnaturally still air and a harsh light. There, leaning against a wooden rack, was Napoleon on St Helena; a thin and rather petulant-looking man with long spindly legs, who stands with his arms folded across his chest, surrounded by a swirling mist of blood red and sun yellow paint. He is staring down into a red haze of shallow water in which he can see his own reflection and the little spinning-top shape of a rock limpet. Behind him there is an English soldier standing on guard, and in the distance you can see Jamestown: a medieval city that has been built along the upper rim of a high cliff so that it looks rather like the town of Bastia in Corsica, or perhaps the monastery of Mount Athos in Greece.

At the National Army Museum they have a big display called The Battle of Waterloo: a bumpy green counterpane divided up into fields on which 70,000 painted tin soldiers, their horses and their cannons, are set out in neat geometric patterns, waiting for the order that will throw one army against the other. In an adjoining room they have a stuffed cat called Crimean Tom which was apparently the only living thing to survive the attack on the city of Sebastopol, and near to him there is the skeleton of Napoleon's favourite horse which was captured at Waterloo and now stands in a glass case, small and naked-looking with nothing to shelter its thin bones. In the library I was shown the visitors' book. It has lost its front cover, but on the spine you can still read, 'Napoleon's Tomb, St Helena, Visitors' Signature Book, 1836–183 '; the final number has been broken off with a flake of the leather binding. It was an odd document, each page thick with a tangle of signatures, dates and comments, all seeming to be written with the same pen and the same faded brown ink. William Mitchell from the ship *Ellen* suggested enigmatically, 'When you visit the tomb of Napoleon, be sure to come early and gallop all the way.' William and Elizabeth Higgarth from Virginia wanted to know 'How soon we may follow him to the long home and may God prepare us for the solemn change.' Joseph Scott 'visited the tomb of the World's Almost Imperial Lord on October 20 1836' and Charles Alexander Gordon of Calcutta was there in September of that same year, 'on a rainy day'. Joshua Bennett was 'homeward bound from the Tristran whaling grounds with 1,100 lbs of Oil', while many Frenchmen made the journey as a pilgrimage, bringing with them their carefully prepared poems, filled with sighs and tears and thoughts about life, death and destiny.

Although the Valley of the Tomb must have been a chaotic place with its smashed fences, its broken willow trees, and the steady stream of curious visitors trampling around in small circles, the tomb itself was solid and well-protected and could not be damaged beyond the surface scratchings of names and dates on the stone slabs. However, when the French took Napoleon away with them in 1840 they were so preoccupied with their own task that they left the place as if it had been ransacked by thieves searching for buried treasure. The vault in which the coffins had lain was left open and gaping and next to it was the excavated trench, six feet deep, that had been dug to speed things up in case they could not break through the layer of cement in time. Part of the cage from Longwood New House had been heaved to one side and pulled out of its stone sockets, and some of the top spikes had been sawn off and taken away as souvenirs. There were piles of rubble and heaps of earth and twisted bands of iron fixed in lumps of cement lying all around the tomb, and the earth was rough and uneven where it had been dug for bulbs or taken away in sackloads. When it rained, the empty vault filled up with water and was converted into 'a little bath some eight feet deep', and when the weather was dry, visitors could climb down into the hole where Napoleon had lain by means of a step ladder 'placed there for the purpose'. During some years there was an entrance fee of three shillings and further sums of money were charged for a taste of the water from the famous spring, or for a bottle of it to take home, a sprig of willow, a rose, a handful of earth.

Meanwhile Longwood continued to disintegrate. Ceilings fell on to broken floors; windows and doors collapsed and were left to rot and the partitions that had separated Napoleon's bedroom, bathroom and study disappeared entirely. In 1850 the farmer who leased the building from the government was granted a new lease for the next twenty-two years, and since, as it was apparently said at the time, 'a live pig is considered more profitable than a dead emperor', he was given permission to knock down part of the house in order to obtain materials for repairing the rest of it. But then in the late 1850s the French began to take the first steps towards acquiring Longwood and the tomb and turning them into monuments dedicated to the memory of Napoleon. The American circus owner, P. T. Barnum, was also very interested in the commercial potential of the two sites, and this put the price up considerably, but in 1858, after a great deal of negotiating, it was agreed that 'Longwood House and its adjoining land of about three acres, and the Val Napoleon with an area of thirty acres, would be sold to His Majesty the Emperor of the French [Napoleon III] and His heirs', for the total sum of £7,000.

So then the task begins of trying to reshape the fragile and collapsing structure of a ruined house and a broken tomb, until they have been transformed into the image, not of what they ever were but of what they represent. The house must be made to look exactly as it did when Napoleon occupied it, but without the confusion of damp floors, a leaking roof, a garden with barricades of crumbling earth and rows of dying trees. The empty tomb must be allowed to settle into its own silence and self-absorption until it is as beautiful as an island that has not yet been discovered. The work took a very long time and was often held up for many years at a stretch. In 1869 a group of men under the command of Captain Masselin were busy scratching at the walls of the rooms in search of a fragment of the original paint or a scrap of wallpaper that would reveal a colour or a design that they could copy. They went back to the memoirs written while Napoleon was in residence, trying to work out how the rooms had been divided and how they had looked when they were in use. They dug at what had been the garden hunting for evidence of a path or a covered walkway, a channel of water, a heap of earth, and slowly they reconstructed an approximation of the past. During this same period the tomb was closed off, bricked up and covered with new blank-faced flagstones, and a deep trench lined with dry stones was dug all the way around it to divert the water from the spring and stop the empty vault from being flooded whenever it rained. The area of thirty acres of land that was now a part of France was fenced off, and with the goats and cattle kept at bay it quickly transformed itself into a forest.

Someone wrote a description of going to Longwood in 1885; walking through silent empty rooms with the shutters closed, the doors wide open and no furniture or decoration to be seen anywhere, apart from a little table near the front entrance door on which a visitors' book was placed, and in the drawing-room a wooden balustrade around an altar and a bust of the Emperor standing over the place where he had died. In 1934 some of the Longwood furniture that had been kept at Plantation House was returned and so the billiard table was again set up in the billiard room, and the two dark globes, one of the heavens and one of the earth, could stand like patient servants on either side of the door leading into the drawing-room. It was around this time that the termites came. They had been in and around Jamestown since the 1850s but they had been kept busy eating their way through houses, books and furniture, and they only moved across to the south-east side of the island much later. The termites managed to destroy almost all that was left of the structure of Napoleon's house and that is why the only original features that have survived are the stone front door steps. Longwood began to be entirely rebuilt in the early 1950s, and the old French Consul whom I had expected to meet, walking towards me in his mohair suit, eager to talk of ghosts and the weather, has been busy with aspects of this work since 1956. I imagine that the house as it is now is very much like it was when Napoleon was there, only of course it is much more perfect: a lifesized portrait with eternal youthfulness and every shining hair in place. The new Consul is busy with the garden, slowly working out which trees and plants are able to survive the battering of the Trade Winds, the rain and the sun, and he says that in twenty years it will all be in order, looking exactly as it should.

I never saw what was left of Longwood New House with its Grecian balcony and its fine views out over Deadwood Plain and the dark mountain of the Barn. For a while it was used as a convalescent home for soldiers on their way back from India, and for a few months one of the island's governors stayed there while the drains at Plantation House were being repaired, but apart from that it was left to stand empty. Someone in Jamestown said that it had finally been demolished only a few years ago, but then just before we left the island I was told that this was not true; the building had been converted and was now being used as a slaughterhouse, but by then it was too late for me to go and have a look at it.

Bibliography

My primary source for the history of St Helena has been the Philip Gosse book, *St Helena, 1502–1938*. My primary source for Napoleon's exile and death on the island has been *St Helena*, by Octave Aubry.

Wherever possible I have based my text on contemporary documents and especially on diaries and letters which I have presumed to be the most trustworthy record. However, I do realise that any selection of information about this subject, taken from the huge amount of documentation available, is bound to be a subjective one.

The Lowe Papers are in the British Library Manuscript Department, Add. 20,107–20,240. They comprise 134 volumes of which 88 deal with all aspects of the period of Napoleon's captivity: copies of official and private letters, records of conversations, reports by Orderly Officers at Longwood, inventories of furniture etc.

I have not included detailed source notes in the text, but in cases where only a particular section of a book is relevant I have indicated volume and page numbers in square brackets in this bibliography.

I have tended to use English translations of French publications where available, although in the case of Antommarchi, Las Cases and St Denis I have also referred to the original texts. The translations of the various songs sung by Napoleon are my own.

Many of the books and journals referred to in this bibliography are very hard to come by. The most complete collection is held by The Royal Commonwealth Society Library, London, and by Trevor Hearl, The St Helena Link at the Cheltenham and Gloucester College of Higher

Education. In France I consulted the library of the Musée de l'Armée and the library at the Musée National du Château de Malmaison.

ABELL, Mrs L. E.: *Recollections of the Emperor Napoleon*, London, John Murray, 1944

ALEXANDER, Capt.: 'New Records of Napoleon', [Report on the exhumation, pp. 404–408], *Century Magazine*, London, 1912

ANON, 'by A Bird of Passage': *St Helena*, London, 1865 [the exhumation and the state of Longwood Old House in the 1840s]

ANON, by 'A Gentleman': *A Brief Account of the Island of St Helena*, 1815

ANTOMMARCHI, F.: *The Last Days of Napoleon*, 2nd ed., 2 vols., London, 1826

ARNOTT, Archibald: *An Account of the late illness, disease and post-mortem examination of Napoleon Bonaparte*, London, 1822

ARKIN, Marcus: 'Supplies for Napoleon's jailers: John Company and the Cape – St Helena Trade During the Captivity, 1815–1821', *Archive Yearbook for South African History 1964*, vol. 1, Capetown, 1964

AUBRY, Octave: *St Helena*, trans. Arthur Livingston, London, Gollancz, 1937

BARNES, J.: *A tour through the island of St Helena; with notices of its geology, mineralogy, botany & etc, collected during a residence of (12) years; with some particulars of Napoleon*, London, 1817

BEATSON, Alex: *Tracts relative to the island of St Helena*, London, 1816

BENNETT, George Brooks: *The St Helena Reminiscences (1816–1851)*, ed. with a foreword by Trevor Hearl, Cheltenham, The Trevor Hearl Collection, 1989

Bibliography

BERTRAND, Arthur: *Lettres sur l'expédition de Ste Hélène en 1840*, Paris, 1841

BERTRAND, H. G.: *Napoleon at St Helena: Memoirs of General Bertrand, January to May, 1821*, deciphered and annotated by Fleuriot de Langle, trans. F. Hume, London, 1953

BOURGUIGNON: *Le Retour des Cendres*, Paris, 1943

BROOKE, Thomas H.: *History of St Helena*, 2nd ed. to 1823, London, 1824

BROOKES, Dame Mabel: *St Helena Story*, London, Heinemann, 1960

CAHUET, Alberic: *Après la mort de l'Empereur*, Paris, 1913 [Longwood and the tomb, pp. 295–311]

CANETTI, Elias, *Crowds and Power*, London, Gollancz, 1962

CHAPLIN, Arnold: *A St Helena Who's Who (Napoleonic)*, 2nd revised ed., London, 1919

CLIFFORD, Hugh: 'The Earliest Exile of St Helena' [story of Fernando Lopez] *Blackwoods Magazine*, London, May 1903

CLIFFORD, H. J.: 'A Visit to Longwood', *Cornhill Magazine*, London, November 1899 [pp. 665–75]

COCKBURN, Admiral Sir G.: *Extracts from the Diary of*, London, 1888

COQUEREAU, Abbé Felix: *Souvenirs du voyage au Ste. Hélène*, Paris, 1841

CROSS, Tony: *St Helena*, Newton Abbot, Devon, David and Charles, 1980

DARLING, Andrew: 'Account of Napoleon's funeral and exhumation, from the diaries of', *The Times*, 30 September 1915

DARWIN, Charles: *Diary of the voyage of HMS Beagle*, Cambridge, 1933 [St Helena, 8–13 July 1836]

FORSYTH, William: *History of the Captivity of Napoleon at St Helena, from the letters and journals of the late Lieut-Gen. Sir Hudson Lowe*, 3 vols., London, 1853

Bibliography

GOSSE, Philip: *St Helena 1502–1938,* new edition with introduction by Trevor Hearl, Oswestry, Shropshire, Anthony Nelson, 1990

GOURGAUD, General Baron: *The St Helena Journal,* preface by Hilaire Belloc, London, Bodley Head, 1932

GRANT, B: *A few notes on St Helena and Descriptive Guide,* St Helena, 1883

HAKLUYT SOCIETY NO. 62: *The Commentaries of the Great Alphonso D'Alboquerque,* vol. III, 1880 [Introduction: xxxiv–xxxix; Footnotes pp. 238–40]

HENRY, Walter: *Events of a Military Life,* 2 vols., London, 1843 [St Helena, vol. II, pp. 1–90]

HUBERT, Nicole: 'Le Mobilier de Longwood Hier et Aujourd'hui' *Souvenir Napoleonien,* Paris, March 1981

JACKSON, Basil: *Reminiscences of a Staff Officer,* London, 1877 [the camp at Deadwood, interview with Napoleon, etc. 1816–19]

JACKSON, E.L.: *St Helena, the Historic Island,* London, 1903

JANISCH, H. R.: *Extracts from the St Helena Records,* St Helena, 1885

KEITH, Arthur: 'The History and Nature of Certain Specimens alleged to have been obtained at the post-mortem examination of Napoleon the Great', *British Medical Journal,* London, 11 January 1913

KEMBLE, James: *Gorrequer's Diary, St Helena during Napoleon's Exile,* London, Heinemann, 1969

KITCHING, G. C.: *A Handbook and Gazetteer of the Island of St Helena,* St Helena, 1937 [Trevor Hearl Collection]

LAS CASES, Count de: *Memoirs of the Life, Exile and Conversations of the Emperor Napoleon,* IV vols., London, 1836

LOCKWOOD, J.: *A Guide to St Helena, Descriptive and Historical, with a Visit to Longwood and Napoleon's Tomb,* St Helena, 1851 [pp. 76–106]

LUTYENS, Major E.: *Letters of Captain Engelbert Lutyens (Orderly Officer at Longwood),* Sir Lees Knowles, 1915

Bibliography

[Includes letters of Ensign Duncan Darroch to his mother, describing Napoleon's death bed, grave etc.]

MALCOLM, Lady: *A Diary of St Helena*, London, 1899

MARCHAND, Louis: *Mémoires*, Paris, 1955

MARTINEAU, Gilbert: *Napoleon's St Helena*, trans. Frances Partridge, London, John Murray, 1968

—— *Napoleon's Last Journey*, trans. Frances Partridge, London, John Murray, 1976

MASSON, Frédéric: *Napoleon at St Helena, 1815–1821*, trans. Louis B. Frewer, Oxford, 1949

MELLIS, J. C.: *St Helena: a physical, historical and topographical description*, London, 1875

MEYNELL, Henry: *Conversations with Napoleon at St Helena*, London, 1911

MONTHOLON, Comte de, *History of the Captivity*, IV vols., London, 1876

MONTHOLON, Comtesse de: *Souvenirs de Ste Hélène, 1815–1816*, Paris, 1901

MUNDY, Capt.: *Pen and Pencil Sketches: The Journal of a Tour in India*, II vols., 2nd ed., London, 1833 [Longwood and the Tomb before the exhumation, vol. II, pp. 343–64]

O'MEARA, Barry: *Exposition of the Transactions that have taken place at St Helena*, London, 1819

—— *Napoleon in Exile or A Voice from St Helena*, II vols., London, 1822

PARK, Julian: *Napoleon in Captivity. The reports of Count Balmain, Russian Commissioner on the island of St Helena 1816–1820*, Trans. and Ed. J. Park, London, Allen and Unwin, 1928

PRIOR, J: *Voyage along the Eastern Coast of Africa . . . to St Helena*, London, 1819

RUSSELL, Lady Constance: *Swallowfield and its Owners*, London, 1901 [Sir Henry Russell's reminiscences of St Helena and Napoleon, pp. 273–93]

ST DENIS, Louis Étienne: *From the Tuileries to St Helena:*

Personal Recollections of Louis Étienne St Denis. Trans.
Frank Hunter Potter, London, 1922

SHORTER, Clement: *Napoleon and his Fellow Travellers*
(including William Warden's *Letters from St Helena*),
London, 1908

STOKOE, John: *With Napoleon at St Helena*. Trans. Edith S.
Stokoe, London, Bodley Head, 1902

VACQUIER, J.: *Authentic Relics of Napoleon I*, Musée de
l'Armée, Paris, 1927

VALENTIA, Lord: *Voyages and Travels* (vol. I), London,
1809

VIGNALI: *Catalogue of Printed Books and Manuscripts in the
Vignali Collection of Napoleonic Relics Removed from St
Helena*, Christie's, Manson and Woods, 29 October
1969

WALLACE, Alfred Russel: *Island Life. The Phenomena and
Causes of Insular Fauna and Flora*, 2nd ed., London, 1892

WATSON, G. L. de St M: *The Story of Napoleon's Death
Mask*, London, Bodley Head, 1915

WINCHESTER, Simon: *Outposts. Journeys to the surviving
relics of the British Empire*, London, Hodder and
Stoughton, 1985

YOUNG, Gavin: *Slow Boats Home*, London, Hutchinson,
1985

YOUNG, Norwood: *Napoleon in Exile: St Helena*, II vols.,
London, 1915

YOUNGHUSBAND, Mrs R.: 'Letters from St Helena',
Blackwoods Magazine, London, August 1947, pp. 144–53